Dialogue in Islam
Qur'an - Sunnah - History

The Dialogue Society is a registered charity, established in London in 1999, with the aim of advancing social cohesion by connecting communities through dialogue. It operates nation-wide with regional branches across the UK. Through localised community projects, discussion forums and teaching programmes it enables people to venture across boundaries of religion, culture and social class. It provides a platform where people can meet to share narratives and perspectives, discover the values they have in common and be at ease with their differences.

www.DialogueSociety.org

info@dialoguesociety.org

Tel: +44 (0)20 7619 0361

Dialogue Society

402 Holloway Road
London N7 6PZ

**DIALOGUE
SOCIETY**

LONDON 1999

Registered Charity No: 1117039

Dialogue in Islam
Qur'an - Sunnah- History

First published in Great Britain 2012

© Dialogue Society 2011

ISBN 978-0-9569304-3-9

About the authors

Ahmet Kurucan was born in 1961 in the city of Tavsanli, Kutahya, Turkey, where he completed his basic education before moving to Ankara to study Theology at Ankara University. Between 1985 and 1988 he received specialised personal tuition from Fethullah Gülen in the Islamic sciences of *fiqh*, *hadith* and *tafsir*. He was later appointed as a preacher by the Presidency of Turkish Religious Affairs and served in several major cities including Izmir and Istanbul until moving on in 1995 to work for the Turkish daily Zaman.

During his time at Zaman, he served as Editorial Coordinator, Publications Editor and Adviser, and worked on the Academy section which hosts religious and cultural issues. He then went on to complete his PhD on freedom of thought in Islam at Ataturk University, Erzurum, in 2006. He currently lives in the USA and works as an adviser for a publishing company. He also contributes to Zaman on a weekly basis, something he began to do during his time with the paper. He is married with three children and is the author of twelve books.

Mustafa Kasim Erol graduated from the Department of Theology, Selcuk University, Turkey. He obtained an MA in Islamic Studies from Birmingham University in 1999. He taught Religious Education and Citizenship in various schools from 2002 to 2008, his most recent teaching post being at Alexandra High School, Birmingham. He was a founding member of several educational organisations and has acted as chairman for some of them in the United Kingdom. He worked for an interfaith NGO in Turkey between 2008 and 2010 and has also worked part time as an Examiner and Team Leader at Cambridge University (2002-present).

In 2011 Mustafa Kasim Erol became the Director of the new Oxford Branch of the Dialogue Society. He is also a full-time PhD Candidate at Kings College, University of London, at the Department of Education and Professional Studies. His areas of interest include Islamic theology, intercultural and interfaith dialogue, education, and human rights. He regularly speaks at conferences and public events on such topics in the UK and overseas. He is married and has 2 children.

Contents

Chapter 3 – The Basis from the Prophet's Life

Chapter 4 – The Historical Basis

Appendices

Acknowledgements

We would like to thank Ozcan Keles for his valuable input to the content of this book; Dr. Jamil Qureshi for his constructive comments and advice on the presentation of the argument; and Frances Sleap for her contribution to the editing and proof-reading of the text. Needless to say, we take full responsibility for any errors or shortcomings that remain in the work.

Foreword

The Dialogue Society was founded by Muslims born and raised in Britain who believe that their faith teaches and requires positive engagement, solidarity and integration with people of different faiths and cultures. Though neither conceived nor run as an Islamic or otherwise religious organisation, the Society was established by people who engage in dialogue because of, not in spite of, their being Muslims, who have a genuine commitment to the goal of respectful and peaceful co-existence within a culturally and confessionally diverse society. I welcome this book as an introduction to the theological necessity, merits and virtue of dialogue in Islam.

As the book's first chapter explains, dialogue is much broader in scope than interfaith or theological conversations and conferences, although these are an important (and worthwhile) dimension of it. The 'dialogue approach' could be thought of as a positive disposition to others being (and remaining) others, which encourages the virtues of neighbourliness, friendship and mutual trust and caring. The authors offer this very useful working definition of dialogue: 'meaningful interaction and exchange between people of different groups (social, cultural, political and religious) who come together through various kinds of conversations or activities with a view to increased understanding.'

This book sets out the reasoning behind the effort to engage and understand. It shows how the Qur'an, Sunnah and Islamic history endorse and indeed require dialogue. Even a cursory acquaintance with the Qur'an tells us that (to my knowledge, uniquely among the major Scriptures) it explicitly conceives of religion in the plural, promising a just reward to all who believe in God and the Last Day and strive to do good in the world. Humankind are different in their religions and races and nations and life-ways; these differences are to be accepted and valued as a means of people being intelligible to one another. Similarly in the Qur'an we find reiterated emphasis on the intelligibility of natural phenomena, and this intelligibility is integral to the utility and beauty of the world, prepared for humankind so that they can prove and improve their worth.

That emphasis explains the extraordinary effort of people in the first centuries of Islam to go out across the world, as scholars and explorers, to record the geography and history, arts and techniques, philosophical and religious ideas, social, commercial and political customs of non-Muslims within and beyond the territories ruled by Muslims. The effort was accompanied by the transportation of diverse goods, crops and technologies from as far away as China and the southern fringes of Scandinavia; and by the translation of seminal works from the languages of India, Persia (Iran) and the Hellenic world of the Mediterranean. At the same time, confidence in the intelligibility of natural phenomena inspired close observation, classification and experimentation which, as is now generally acknowledged, laid the foundations of modern scientific reasoning and investigation of the natural world. Throughout this period, the contribution of non-Muslims at the very highest levels of scholarship, government and administration, and commercial enterprise, was conspicuous and accepted as normal and natural. Of course, as we accept, there was a falling off from the ideals of that richly diverse multi-ethnic and multicultural Islamic civilisation.

This book is a reminder that the momentum that engendered that civilisation came from the sources that are still accepted as marking the inner and outer horizons of being a Muslim. Those sources are the Qur'an and the Sunnah. The authors demonstrate that dialogue (understood as meaningful engagement with people of different outlooks and backgrounds) is a part of the fabric of Islam, embedded in its very foundation. It is not just something that is encouraged as either an optional good, or as a temporary posture necessitated by the status of being a minority or being politically weak. Rather, it is required by the innate disposition with which God endowed all human beings, and it is required by fundamental Islamic principles of conduct derived from mainstream, long-established understanding of the commands of the Qur'an and Sunnah. Accordingly, being a good Muslim requires responding positively to diversity and being proactively engaged in wider society.

The arguments presented in this book are not based on a sectarian or minority opinion. They adduce the mainstream sources of religious teaching on Islam and use the mainstream methods applied to those sources. Indeed, the vast majority of Muslims across the world believe that positive engagement with the different cultural and religious groups in a society is a cornerstone teaching of Islam. What is more, this fundamental teaching is not looked upon as an abstract or unattainable ideal. Rather, it is part of the everyday practice of Muslim neighbourliness in different communities world-wide, wherever that practice is not wilfully blocked by armed conflicts.

Also, dialogue is being put into practice by thousands of Islamically-inspired dialogue organisations across the world. Their understanding of the teachings of Qur'an and Sunnah motivates their commitment to dialogue projects and shapes the spirit of respect, hospitality and generosity in which they seek to engage with diverse groups. In turn their experience contributes to a deeper understanding and fuller interpretation of those Islamic teachings related to dialogue. Through projects which bring people of diverse cultural backgrounds together, fostering good will, trust and co-operation, they witness and experience just how much can be learned, shared and achieved when different communities get to know one another. Islamically-inspired leaders of dialogue thereby enter into a more profound appreciation of the divine purpose in human diversity, as expressed in *al-Hujurat*, 49:13. In responding faithfully to the teachings of the Qur'an and Sunnah and actively seeking peaceful, just relationships with diverse groups, they begin to learn experientially what faithfulness to the commands of the Qur'an and the example of the Prophet, peace be upon Him (pbuh) really means in the context of intercultural engagement.

This book is an introduction to the material in Islamic sources relevant to dialogue. As such, it should first of all be of interest to Muslims, like myself, born and raised in the West. For us, who live in a society where the dominant influences come from people of other faiths and backgrounds, including people of no faith at all, it is important to understand the Islamic basis for dialogue. It becomes all the more important when we Muslims, among others, are being targeted by extremists of all kinds who favour confrontation in place of co-existence, hatred and suspicion in place of good will and trust. I write this foreword just months after a massacre fuelled by xenophobic right-ring extremism claimed seventy-seven lives in Norway. In the face of the rise of such extremism, and of further so-called 'religiously motivated' terror plots in the UK, it is indispensable that people of diverse cultural and religious backgrounds stand together in solidarity and actively cultivate relationships of understanding, respect and peace.

I am pleased to note that, like its argument, the language and style of this book are inclusive, so that what it says can be read with equal benefit by specialists and non-specialists, Muslims and non-Muslims.

In the spirit of dialogue I invite readers to send me any comments, critical or otherwise, on the ideas and arguments set forth in this book: email to dialogueinislam@dialoguesociety.org.

Ozcan Keles
Executive Director

Dialogue Society
London, January 2012

Preface

The existence of social groups that differ on the basis of race, tribe, nationality or religion carries the potential of competition and conflict between them. There exist many different communities of believers with their distinctive religions, prophets and sacred scriptures. This plurality is both a reason for and an outcome of the human freedom to choose faith and religion, the basis of moral responsibility and final judgement. In this respect religious plurality is one of the means to test and develop human capacities. People are required to overcome inter-group tensions and their potential negative outcomes through good will and the commitment to live together in peace and justice with their fellow human beings, whatever the odds. In other words, the response to diversity through positive engagement or dialogue is one of the major goals that the divine will has set for humankind.

The larger part of this book is taken up with reflection on the teachings of the Qur'an and the example, precepts and practice of the Prophet (pbuh) (hereafter, the Sunnah) relevant to the practice of dialogue, and on the light shed on dialogue by Islamic history. Prior to this reflection, in Chapter 1, we examine the meaning of dialogue as understood by key theorists and by practitioners. We distinguish dialogue from debate and discussion, and clarify the meaning of interfaith dialogue. What is being argued for in this book, on the basis of Islamic sources, is not theological engagement with people of different faiths but general meaningful engagement with diverse groups. Accordingly, our working definition of dialogue is: **meaningful interaction and exchange between people of different groups (social, cultural, political and religious) who come together through various kinds of conversations or activities with a view to increased understanding.**

Chapter 2, focused on relevant material from the Qur'an, begins with a discussion of its particular instructions to Muslims to engage positively with the People of the Book, that is, those 'others' who align themselves with prophets recognised by Muslims. We then move on to discussion of verses relevant to dialogue with people of any faith, or none. It is worthwhile briefly

to note some of the key verses here, as they encapsulate the Qur'an's challenge
to Muslims to accept diversity and to respond to it with righteousness and
justice:

> Say, 'Now the truth has come from your Lord: let those who
> wish to believe in it do so, and let those who wish to reject it do
> so.' (al-Kahf, 18:29)

> There is no compulsion in religion. (al-Baqarah, 2:256)

> Had your Lord willed, all the people on earth would have
> believed. So can you [O Prophet] compel people to believe?
> (Yunus, 10:99)

> If God so willed, He would have made you all one people.
> (al-Nahl, 16:93)

What we learn from these verses is that diversity was intended by God
and that it is not possible that everyone in the world will believe in the
same religion. This requires us to learn how to live together, which in turn
necessitates dialogue. The following verses from the Qur'an show us the
divine wisdom in such diversity, encouraging us to engage:

> O people, We created you all from a single man and a single
> woman, and made you into races and tribes so that you should
> get to know one another. In God's eyes, the most honoured of
> you are the ones most mindful of Him: God is all knowing, all
> aware. (al-Hujurat, 49:13)

> We have assigned a law and a path to each of you. If God had
> so willed, He would have made you one community, but He
> wanted to test you through that which He has given you, so race
> to do good: you will all return to God and He will make clear to
> you the matters you differed about. (al-Ma'ida, 5:48)

> If your Lord had pleased, He would have made all people a
> single community, but they continue to have their differences
> – except those on whom your Lord has mercy – for He created
> them to be this way. (Hud, 11:118–19)

In Chapter 2 we also reflect on verses which, on a superficial reading, might be construed as opposing dialogue. With reference to their occasions of revelation we consider the implications of these verses for Muslims living in different eras and circumstances. We argue that the verses concerned with struggle against Jews, Christians or polytheists do not govern our relations with any and all people belonging to these religions in any and all circumstances; rather, they govern our relationships with only those people who follow the practice of those Jews, Christians and polytheists who actively threatened the security of the Muslims when the verses were revealed. That is how the verses were understood at the time, and that is how that understanding was embodied in practice for centuries afterwards. In this chapter we also explain that there is no contradiction between the concepts of *jihād* and of dialogue if each is properly understood.

Chapter 3, on the basis for dialogue provided by the life of the Prophet (pbuh), explores examples of the courtesy, respect, justice and compassion that he displayed in his dealings with people of other faiths and cultures. We give special attention to the Medina Charter, through which the Prophet (pbuh) secured political and legal arrangements facilitating peace, co-operation and trust between diverse religious and cultural groups. The Prophet (pbuh) entered into a range of other agreements with individuals and groups of different religions, as well as entering into social and commercial relations with various individual Jews and Christians. We give a range of examples of the justice and generosity he showed in all these relationships, and which serve as a model for all Muslims in their dealings with people of other faiths and diverse cultures. We also elucidate the contexts in which the Prophet (pbuh) had to fight or punish people of other religions, explaining the implications of these incidents in different political and social conditions.

Chapter 4 briefly considers what can be learnt from the application of the religious teaching of Qur'an and Sunnah in the practice of the Four Righteous Caliphs and, after them, of the Umayyads, Abbasids, Seljuks and Ottomans, in their dealings with non-Muslims living under Muslim rule. We give examples of compassion, justice and respect shown to non-Muslims in particular historical incidents and in agreements entered into by Muslim rulers. We note the general faithfulness of early Muslim rulers to the principle that 'there is no compulsion in religion.' We also briefly clarify the nature of the treaties which granted protection and religious freedom to non-Muslim subjects of the Islamic state.

In the very different contemporary world Muslims must still respond to the challenges of pluralism and diversity. The Qur'an and Sunnah demand that Muslims engage in dialogue. The reality of globalisation makes that demand all the more pressing. The rapidly improving technologies of communication and transportation are turning the world into a global neighbourhood and this process is accelerating, with new dimensions of interconnection continually being opened up. In today's world, Muslims, Christians, Buddhists, Hindus and Jews are not clearly separated either by geographic location or by different political allegiances. We need to be aware of these changed realities. If we maintain an attitude in the present time as if we were living centuries ago, we will be depriving ourselves of the opportunity to sustain the relevance of Islam amid present realities and isolating ourselves from the rest of the world. We have to learn to co-exist successfully with all of those with whom we share this world. The isolation of the Muslim *ummah* (community), its separation from people of different creeds and cultures, is undesirable from a religious perspective; it is also impossible in the global neighbourhood the world is increasingly becoming.

Therefore we Muslims have to make our presence felt, take our place at the forums where global affairs are discussed and be a party to decision-making processes in our shared world. As Muslims, drawing on our shared religious values as well as our distinctive and diverse national and cultural values, we can make a significant and positive contribution to the discussions and decisions that affect all of us.

As Muslims, it is our duty to enter into relations with others on the pattern set by the Prophet (pbuh). We are responsible for applying the example of the Prophet's (pbuh) life as a whole in our own lives since he is our guide and model. Taking only his prayers or his relationship with Muslims into account would mean that we narrow or even betray our religion by adopting only what suits us and ignoring the rest. We need also to mirror his example of truthfulness and trustworthiness in his dealings with all people.

We have not attempted a comprehensive discussion of all the material from the Qur'an, the Sunnah and Islamic history relevant to dialogue. Our more modest aim was to present the main arguments for dialogue from those sources and address the main objections to dialogue and positive engagement. For the sake of clarity and ease of reading, we have made every effort to avoid technical terms and to keep footnotes to the absolute minimum. Wherever possible, we have put things in plain English, with the precise Arabic term in parenthesis – there is in any case a Glossary of such terms at the end of this book. Also, we have arranged the material, to the extent possible, in sections that can be read independently.

For the sake of consistency we have used the same translation of the Qur'an throughout. We settled on the recent translation by M. A. S. Abdel-Haleem (Oxford University Press, 2010), which has been widely praised for the clarity and accessibility of its language.

Ahmet Kurucan and Mustafa Kasim Erol
January 2012

Chapter 1

About Dialogue

What is dialogue?

The root of the word *dialogue* (from the Greek *dialogos*, from *dia*, across, and *legein*, to speak) tells us that it is the effort to share meaning with someone. By intercultural or interfaith dialogue we mean a conversation between different individuals or groups whose purpose is simply honest engagement and increased mutual understanding. This kind of dialogue can be distinguished from debate, where we seek to win an argument, to persuade others of our point of view. It is also different from discussion, which aims to solve a problem, reach a consensus or decide on a course of action. In dialogue we engage with others for the sake of engagement; we are looking simply for meaningful human interaction through which we may grow in understanding of the other, of ourselves and of the relationship between us.

Various philosophers and social scientists have reflected on dialogue, and offered their own detailed ideas and theories about it. The twentieth-century philosopher Martin Buber[1] saw true dialogue as a kind of interaction that provides understanding through direct experience of the other. He saw it as a genuine, transformative encounter between the participants seeing and responding to each other as persons, not as 'things' that they might use as means to an end. For Buber, dialogue is a deeply meaningful interpersonal experience which can change you, as it can help you see yourself from the perspective of the other.

David Yankelovich, whose book *The Magic of Dialogue*[2] explores dialogue's potential to transform conflict into co-operation, describes dialogue as a conversation under three particular conditions:

- equality (or at least suspension, as far as humanly possible, of inequality and coercive influences);

---

1   Martin Buber, *I and Thou*, (New York: Simon and Schuster, 1971), 62 ff.

2   Daniel Yankelovich, *The Magic of Dialogue*, (New York: Simon and Schuster, 1999), 41 ff.

- listening with empathy in order to understand, and

- bringing assumptions out into the open.

These conditions are undoubtedly helpful in facilitating the sort of genuine human encounter that Buber envisioned, in which we meet the other as a valued human person, setting aside power games and the impulse to control or use others for our ends. Through the effort to meet as equals, to listen with empathy, and to be open about our preconceptions and prejudices, we may break down some of the barriers in the way of meaningful human interaction. For dialogue practitioners, the full achievement of all three conditions is perhaps something to aspire to: an ideal set of circumstances in which a really profound dialogue may take place.

David Bohm, one of the most interesting and influential contemporary theorists in this area, highlighted the range of learning that can take place in dialogue.[3] He promoted the practice of dialogue as a completely free-flowing conversation, without restrictions on the themes explored or the outcomes of the discussion. In a group engaging in this kind of dialogue, he suggested, people can better understand not only the positions of all the participants (including themselves) on the matters talked about, but also their emotions, preconceptions, prejudices and desires. They are able to do this by paying attention to the contributions of all participants and to their own intellectual and emotional responses. This kind of dialogue, in which participants make a conscious effort to examine the emotional dynamics of the conversation and their own responses, can provide an ideal context for achieving genuine human encounter; identifying the mental and emotional baggage that people are carrying often allows them to see beyond it and start to see others more accurately and empathetically.

While philosophical and social theorists who give definitions of dialogue often keep to its literal meaning and interpret it in terms of verbal communication, practitioners of intercultural and interfaith dialogue tend to use the word in a broader sense. For them, and for us in this book, the key idea is that of *engagement*. We can meet and better understand different individuals or groups not only through focused verbal conversations but in all sorts of other ways, formal and informal. We can interact meaningfully with

---

3   David Bohm, *On Dialogue*, (Abingdon, Oxon: Routledge, 2004), 6ff, 79ff; David Bohm, Donald Factor and Peter Garrett, *Dialogue, a Proposal*, (1991), http://www.david-bohm.net/dialogue/dialogue_proposal.html.

others through, for example, social events like sharing a meal, or working co-operatively on voluntary projects for the common good. Throughout this book we understand and use the term dialogue in this broad, inclusive sense, which we can sum up in this way:

> Dialogue consists of meaningful interaction and exchange between people of different groups (social, cultural, political and religious) who come together through various kinds of conversations or activities with a view to increased understanding.

The argument of this book is that an Islamic understanding of human nature, the teachings of the Qur'an and the Sunnah, and examples from Islamic history, all require that Muslims engage in a positive manner with their fellow human beings from different cultural and religious groups. Once this is established, it is up to individual Muslims to explore the many ways, informal or organised, in which they can take part in dialogue, and how the experience of engaging with people of other faiths and cultures can enrich their experience as Muslims.

Dialogue is often associated with particular social goals, such as improving relations between different groups or even helping to resolve conflicts. But we hold that the primary reason for engaging in dialogue is that it is *inherently valuable*. If it can sometimes address conflicts and tension this is to be welcomed, but it is secondary. Dialogue is a good in itself, quite apart from any social or other goods that may flow from it.

Dialogue is a natural manifestation of our humanness, as both the Qur'an and the life of the Prophet (pbuh) make clear. The Qur'an tells us that the fundamental oneness of all human beings and their ethnic and linguistic plurality together enable us to engage with and understand one another:

> People, We created you all from a single man and a single woman, and made you into races and tribes so that you should get to know one another... (*al-Hujurat*, 49:13)

Accounts of Prophet Muhammad's (pbuh) life show that he was a model of positive engagement with those around him before he was called to be a prophet, since before that time he was known as *al-Sadiq al-Amin*, 'the truthful and the trustworthy.' Thus at that time he positively engaged with others not in obedience to the revealed word of God (Qur'an) but in obedience to the norms of God's creation – the innate disposition (*fitra*) with which God endowed all human beings. As Fethullah Gülen says, we must consider ourselves human first from the point of view of our nature and responsibilities, before we consider our belonging to a religious or cultural tradition. Our fundamental God-given human disposition turns us towards positive engagement with other human beings; it turns us towards dialogue. This is underlined by various peculiarities of our biological and spiritual make-up. The striking concentration of over fifty muscles in the human face gives us scope for subtle and effective communication through facial expressions before we even use any words. We also find in ourselves, if we are open to this element of our human make-up, a great capacity for communication with God and with others at a profound spiritual level.

The inherent value of dialogue becomes clearer when we recognise that the creation is intelligible, enabling and requiring us to be responsive to it, to engage with it materially, intellectually and spiritually. As Said Nursi stated, 'Beauty and fairness desire to see and be seen. Both of these require the existence of yearning witnesses and bewildered admirers.'[4] God created intelligent beings to seek Him and respond to Him. While angels share this role, human beings are in the unique position of having free choice; we can freely choose to worship and obey our Creator and so can engage with Him in a unique way.

God's will that human beings seek Him and respond to His creation and His will is indicated by the appearance of thousands of prophets and messengers over the course of human history. In addition, through select messengers He sent books explaining His will and the human role in His creation. Further, God's creative action is continuous and ongoing; through the events which he brings about in the created world He engages with, teaches and communicates with us. And He calls us to respond actively and regularly through prayer and service; this is our God-appointed purpose:

> I created jinn and mankind only to worship Me. (*al-Dhariyat*, 51:56)

Worship itself is a form of dialogue with God. What is more, worshiping

---

4   B. Said Nursi, *The Words*, trans. Şükran Vahide, (İstanbul: Sözler Publications, 1993), 80.

God requires us to know God, within the narrow limits of our human capacities. Knowing God requires exploration, contemplation and enquiry. This makes it necessary for us to engage with the world and with others, to see the hand of the Creator in the created. As such, we are made for dialogue with God as well as with each other.

What is interfaith dialogue?

'Dialogue between followers of different faith traditions' would be a more correct expression than 'interfaith dialogue', because it is individuals of faith who engage with each other, not entire 'faiths'. However, the term 'interfaith dialogue' is already in widespread use to mean dialogue between followers of different faiths, and so we will use it in this sense also.

Dialogue between followers of different faiths gives them the opportunity to talk to and listen to each other, getting to know and learning to understand the 'other'. In interfaith dialogue we try to approach our partners in a spirit of tolerance, truthfulness, sincerity, love, respect and good will, without willing the other to accept our own beliefs or ideas.

As we explained above in distinguishing dialogue from debate and discussion, in dialogue we are not aiming either to win an argument or to establish a consensus. We are engaging for the sake of engaging, seeking a genuine encounter with other human beings in accordance with our God-given capacities for engagement and communication. In interfaith dialogue we look to interact with people of different faiths, gaining understanding of their faith and other aspects of their identities, as well as improving our understanding of our own.

What (interfaith) dialogue is not

It is important here to make clear what dialogue, and particularly interfaith dialogue, is not. Dialogue is not debate; it is not about convincing others of one's position, or trying to win an argument. Nor is it about compromise. In a dialogue people are *not* aiming to agree on everything or to reach a consensus. Dialogue is simply about honest engagement and communication, in which we try to better understand the other, whatever the differences in our beliefs and values.

Interfaith dialogue does not compromise one's own faith. Throughout the dialogue process, everyone holds to the values that they believe in; and they do not hesitate to implement all of their religious, moral, and cultural values and acts of worship in their lives. Because dialogue is not about trying to win an argument nobody engaged in interfaith dialogue should be trying to disprove the religion of others. Similarly, because dialogue is not about establishing a consensus, nobody should be trying to merge distinct religions into one. It is crucial to dialogue that disagreement and diversity are accepted and respected. The integrity of each belief system involved should not be undermined. Participants can remain faithful to their own beliefs and values while working to understand those of others and to discover and underline the values they share.

Someone who is secure in their own faith need not fear that it will be shaken by dialogue. People do not fall away from their faith simply through honest communication with others. Their faith will only be vulnerable if they are not fully committed to their religious values and if these values do not satisfy their needs. There are very few former Muslims who have converted out of Islam as a result of dialogue with people of other religions. If people feel uncertain about their own faith and identity this may not be the best time for them to engage in certain forms of dialogue, which may confuse their efforts to establish their beliefs and values. There would be no harm in such people engaging in sociable intercultural activities, but they may want to avoid in-depth discussions of faith until they have developed a firmer hold on their own religious identity.

Interfaith dialogue as we understand means dialogue between people of different faiths, not specifically dialogue about faiths. It is entirely possible to engage in interfaith dialogue without broaching theological issues. Interfaith dialogue might, for example, consist of discussion of a pressing social issue amongst local Muslims and Christians; or it might consist of the natural conversational exchange between Buddhists and Jews during an interfaith trip to a historic site.

In interfaith dialogue we should communicate with the other honestly and compassionately. In doing so we express our God-given capacity for interpersonal engagement and we strive to understand one another and learn how to live together harmoniously. In the context of interfaith dialogue we should not be attempting to demonstrate the superiority of our faith or to proselytise in any way. Interfaith dialogue is not to be confused with Islamic *tabligh* (preaching or presenting Islam) or Christian missionary work. We do not mean to suggest that there is anything wrong with preaching to bring others to Islam; we simply mean that interfaith dialogue is not the appropriate forum for that. 'Dialogue', as outlined above, has a particular meaning. Fethullah Gülen describes it as, 'an endeavour to get to know each other and a common search for solutions to our shared problems by accepting everyone in their own position.'[5] To go into dialogue with the intention of converting others would be to serve an agenda at odds with the generally accepted purpose of the dialogue. Indeed, it would be dishonest.

Some people might see this as theologically problematic. Here, it must suffice to mention the social and cultural dimensions of freedom of religion and belief (hereinafter abbreviated to 'freedom of religion'). Freedom of religion involves the four elements of freedom to believe in any religion, to practise its values, to communicate them to others, and to associate and organise with one's fellow believers. Freedom of religion obtains only where and when all four elements are in place. The lack of one of those elements in any country means that there is a lack of freedom of religion there. Achieving this minimum level of freedom of religion is a must. The individuals and organisations that wish to openly promote their religion should be able to do so through the institutionalisation of freedom of religion. In some countries around the world, including Britain, freedom of religion is embedded in the legal-administrative system (in the Human Rights Act in the case of the United Kingdom). As a result, Muslims, Jews, Hindus, Buddhists, and others are able to practise and teach their religious and cultural values and to organise even though they are minorities.

Entering into dialogue with people of different beliefs does not mean that we surrender or compromise our own. It does not even mean that we forgo our right to proselytise in a different context. It only means that we respect that they have the right to believe in and practise their religion, just as we do. Dialogue is a context in which we express our support for the same universal religious freedom that would allow us, in other contexts, to seek to spread our own faith without fear of persecution.

---

5   Fethullah Gülen, *Gurbet Ufukları*, (İstanbul: Gazeteciler ve Yazarlar Vakfı, 2004), 73.

What can dialogue achieve?

Considering the practice of dialogue from a Muslim's perspective, the first question we should ask is whether or not it is necessitated by religion. If the answer is 'Yes', then the question of its utility is secondary. The answer to that question lies in three primary sources: the word of God in the Qur'an, the example of the Prophet (pbuh) and the norms of God's creation (*Sunnatullah*). On all counts we affirm that dialogue is a religious duty for Muslims. (More detailed consideration of these sources will come in the next chapters.)

Once it has been established that religion requires dialogue, we can consider the secondary question of its effects. What does dialogue achieve?

There are a number of valuable benefits. If we agree that dialogue is a religious requirement then dialogue contributes to the fulfilment of our religion. If we agree that dialogue is a natural expression of our innate human disposition (*fitra*), then dialogue enriches our experience as human beings.

Dialogue can enhance our understanding of ourselves because, by contextualising ourselves among others who are different, we see our own beliefs, values and identities more clearly. If we lay a coloured shape on a background of a different, contrasting colour, it stands out much more clearly. In the same way, when we explore our own beliefs and values in the context of different ones, we see more clearly what is distinctive in our own identity, as well as learning to appreciate what is distinctive about others. Far from threatening or undermining our religious identity, dialogue can affirm it and bring us a more profound appreciation of our own faith in all its uniqueness and beauty.

Further, by helping others to better understand who we are and what we stand for, we challenge stereotypes, correct misconceptions and reduce prejudice. In turn we gain understanding of the beliefs and values of those others, which may correct mistakes in our perceptions of them. A great deal of the tension and distrust that sometimes exists between different groups is based on misunderstanding and can be successfully reduced or eliminated through the understanding which dialogue can bring about. Thus dialogue can contribute to stable, peaceful relations between different groups, which is a religious objective apart from anything else.

In addition, dialogue can enable us to explore together solutions to all kinds of shared problems. Today we face global problems such as moral degeneration, environmental pollution, unfair distribution of economic gains, disease, poverty, collapse of family values, fanaticism in the name of race, religion and nationalism, and problems threatening world peace such as terrorism, war and exploitation. Religions and their adherents can contribute to the solutions of these problems, especially when interfaith relations are strong and different groups can trust each other and work together harmoniously. Interfaith and intercultural dialogue helps to make such trust possible.

Can dialogue not be used for other purposes?

A common cause for distrust of dialogue projects is the suspicion that others involved in the dialogue have an ulterior motive and are using it as a cover for proselytism. This suspicion is sometimes connected to particular cases where people have seemed to blur what should be a clear line between dialogue and proselytism.

This suspicion may be linked to collective memories of the nineteenth century when missionaries from Western countries accompanied or followed colonial invaders. The history of that period has inevitably made much of the Muslim world very wary of Christian proselytisers, and of those who might share their aims. Not only did missionaries come to Muslim lands in large numbers with proselytising intentions, they were also inextricably associated with the military force, exploitation and cultural imperialism of that period. For some, collective memories of Christian missionary activity in the context of colonial oppression heighten concerns about any activities that might be a cover for a renewed effort of proselytism. Our purpose here is not to point accusing fingers at the past but to explain why dialogue activities are viewed by some with a degree of apprehension. However, having acknowledged particular historical reasons for some of the reservations that Muslims may feel about dialogue, we maintain that we should not allow ourselves to be ruled by the past.

There can be, and have been, cases where people who claim to want to engage in interfaith dialogue to improve mutual understanding in fact go into it seeking to proselytise. Let us be clear that that is not what this book means by (interfaith) dialogue. Dialogue is one thing, proselytising is another. We do not dispute the universal right of freedom to teach and preach one's religion and to proselytise. However, it is morally completely unacceptable to disguise that as dialogue.

The key point here is that the fact that some people have used dialogue to proselytise does not mean

i) that Muslims do not engage sincerely in dialogue; nor

ii) that all people seeking to engage in dialogue today are 'really' looking to proselytise.

Neither of these statements is true.

Our argument that the first statement is untrue is as follows. First of all, we should arrive at our view of dialogue through consideration of what the primary Islamic sources say on the matter. For an observant Muslim, what the primary sources teach on the matter should be definitive. We affirm, as explained above, that these sources necessitate dialogue. Also, the innate God-given human disposition (*fitra*) necessitates dialogue. Moreover, the God-created laws of causality and utility necessitate dialogue since it is through dialogue that we can 'come to know one another' and establish peaceful relations. So (i) primary Islamic sources, (ii) innate human disposition and (iii) utility, all dictated by God, require dialogue.

As to the second statement, the experience of many Muslims engaged in interfaith dialogue is that the majority of groups from other faiths who participate have a genuine desire to enhance mutual understanding without attempting to proselytise. The desire to promote mutual understanding, eliminate inter-group tensions and secure peace, which motivates Muslims to dialogue, also motivates people of other faiths.

A relationship based on an alert consciousness, serious attention and prior mutual agreement could eliminate all of the articulated and unarticulated concerns that people may feel when entering into interfaith dialogue.

In the regrettable event of any group entering into dialogue with an ulterior motive, this will undoubtedly become clear as the process goes on. In such a case other groups are free to discontinue the dialogue, and would be justified in doing so.

What is the difference between *tabligh* and dialogue?

Tabligh, as popularly understood, is a method of communicating and explaining the faith to others. From this perspective, *tabligh* may be regarded as the counterpart of the work of missionaries in the Western world. But is this really a correct way of understanding what *tabligh* stands for? Religions are broadly either missionary or non-missionary. Islam and Christianity can be called missionary faiths, because they urge their followers actively to disseminate information about their beliefs. However, in both religions, faith can be communicated in a range of different ways.

A number of concepts in the Islamic tradition can be associated with this effort of communication, such as *tabligh, amr bi-l-ma'ruf wa-nahy 'ani l-munkar, da'wah,* and *irshad.* Each of these concepts has a different meaning and a different area of application. Although these concepts are neatly categorised and understood separately in academic circles, the distinctions between them have often become blurred, with their differences not considered and all of them often placed in the category of *tabligh.*

Tabligh literally means to 'convey and transmit something to someone'. Its usage in Islamic terminology connotes expressing the divine message in a wide range of activities that include arts and crafts, dress, lifestyle and manners. *Tabligh* does not mean asserting that Islam is the one true religion and all others are false, and on that narrow basis pressing people to become Muslims. The traditional Islamic ways of sharing the message of Islam are much more subtle and comprehensive than that. Inviting to Islam (for which the usual term is *da'wah*) similarly has its particular traditional methodology and cannot be narrowed to a vulgar imposition of Islam as the one true religion.

There is a clear distinction between these two irreconcilable positions: on the one hand the belief of an individual that their religion's teachings are true and their sincere wish that those teachings be understood and acknowledged, and on the other hand pressing people to become Muslims or abusing their vulnerabilities to force one's faith on them. While the former is a proper sentiment, the latter is completely wrong from an Islamic point of view. According to Islam, one freely chooses to adhere to a faith, in line with the fundamental principle that everyone has the right to believe in the faith of his or her choice without compulsion or coercion of any kind. *Tabligh* is the transmission of Islam's message through example and courteous speech in a manner that fully respects freedom of religion and belief.

As explained above, dialogue consists of meaningful interaction and exchange between individuals of different groups (social, cultural, political and religious) with a view to increased mutual understanding. From a religious perspective, dialogue is the coming together of people of different faiths and convictions without coercion, to learn about each other and perhaps also to discuss common issues in an atmosphere of mutual tolerance, respect and civility.

The goal of dialogue is to increase mutual understanding among the participants. Beyond that, it may also contribute to finding mutually acceptable solutions to shared problems. When dialogue strives for its proper goal, it can help establish respect and understanding in society at large so that group differences do not become a reason for hatred or abuse. In other words, dialogue efforts help establish a culture of peaceful co-existence both in the minds of dialogue participants and in their communities.

Chapter 2

The Qur'anic Basis for Dialogue

What does the Qur'an say about dialogue?

Activities in the name of religion should naturally abide by the commands and prohibitions of religion. For Muslims as a whole the Qur'an is the first primary source for doctrine and norms, a source that is never mistaken and never misguides. Therefore no idea or movement that is not or cannot be endorsed by the Qur'an – no matter when, where, how, why and by whom the ideas or movements are followed – will ever be accepted and welcomed by Muslims as a whole.

The Qur'an's position on interfaith and intercultural dialogue is not immediately clear when we consider all the verses which seem to have a bearing on the issue. There are many verses which require explanation, either because of our ignorance or because they need to be clarified by qualified experts in line with the established methods of Qur'anic exegesis (*tafsir*) that take account of the ways very specific to the Qur'an in which non-Muslims are referred to.

The opponents of interfaith dialogue appeal to a number of verses in support of their position, including those concerning whether or not Jews and Christians are People of the Book, those that command that unbelievers be killed, and those that instruct that Jews and Christians should not be taken as 'friends'. *Jihad* (especially in the its narrowest sense of struggle with groups engaged in active hostilities against the Muslims and Islam) and various practices in Islamic history have also been used to argue that dialogue is un-Islamic.

The verses cited by these opponents of dialogue have to do with regulating the relations of Muslim individuals and societies with People of the Book and with polytheists (*mushriqs*). When we analyse the verses revealed during the Mecca and Medina periods as a whole, we find a nuanced system of classification of non-Muslim groups. These groups include the hypocrites who pretended to be with the Muslims (*munafiqs*) and the polytheists (*mushriqs*), who conspired together against the Muslim society and sought to ruin its political, religious and military relations with non-Muslim groups like the Jews and Christians. It is important to be clear about which verses regulate relations with which kind of group. It is also important to consider which circumstances are regulated by which verses. Some of the verses in question set out rules of conduct towards non-Muslims appropriate during actual hostilities, while others regulate relations with non-Muslims in times of peace. Still others regulate very specific, extraordinary circumstances.

All of the different situations just mentioned are regulated individually by the verses in question. If we do not understand the particular judgements in detail and in their historical context, it is possible to distort their meaning completely. For example, to interpret the verses from an anti-dialogue perspective without knowing which of them applies to a state of war, and which to a state of peace, is to ignore the Qur'an's commands to be fair and just to all, to speak kindly even to those who speak ill of them, etc., and the historical Islamic practice based on those commands. One needs to have knowledge of the methodology of *tafsir* and of the relevant history in order to read and understand the particular verses correctly. Opponents of dialogue have generally interpreted these verses rather superficially, neglecting the different situations they were intended to regulate.

Only exceptionally does the Qur'an make explicit mention of the events or occasions in relation to which certain verses were revealed (*asbab al-nuzul*; sing. *sabab al-nuzul*). We must take account of the wider context (not included in the Qur'an) and of the particular *sabab* of a verse if we are to avoid grave errors of understanding and behaviour.

Proper interpretation of particular verses is also assisted by a holistic approach to the Qur'an. The Qur'an is an entirely internally consistent text. Any apparent contradictions between verses come from faulty interpretation. Interpreters that the Islamic community has deemed credible understand each individual verse in the light of other relevant verses and in accordance with the fundamental messages of the Qur'an.

In this chapter, we try to look at the Qur'an holistically and to give considered interpretations of those verses which at first sight seem to propose an anti-dialogue approach or stance. We show that superficial interpretations by unqualified people indicate just the opposite of the divine will.

We also include the verses that encourage Muslims to engage in dialogue with others, along with their interpretations. The following are a few examples of these verses:

> People, we created you all from a single man and a single woman, and made you into races and tribes so that you should get to know one another. In God's eyes, the most honoured of you are the ones most mindful of Him: God is all knowing, all aware. (*al-Hujurat*, 49:13)

> We have assigned a law and a path to each of you. If God had so willed, He would have made you one community, but He wanted to test you through that which He has given you, so race to do good: you will all return to God and He will make clear to you the matters you differed about. (*al-Ma'ida*, 5:48)

> [Believers], argue only in the best way with the People of the Book, except with those of them who act unjustly. Say, 'We believe in what was revealed to us and in what was revealed to you; our God and your God is one [and the same]; we are devoted to Him.' (*al-'Ankabut*, 29:46)

This last verse is one of several in the Qur'an which encourage respect towards and dialogue with a particular group: the People of the Book. We will begin our exploration of the case for dialogue in the Qur'an by considering its teachings concerning relations with this group. We must therefore first clarify who the People of the Book are.

Who are the People of the Book?

We begin with the People of the Book because the Qur'an, while it supports dialogue in general, makes a particular call to Muslims to engage positively with the People of the Book.

From an Islamic point of view we can distinguish, on the basis of their faith, five groups of people: believers (Muslims), polytheists (*mushriqs*), unbelievers (*kafirs*), hypocrites (*munafiqs*) and People of the Book (*ahl al-kitab*). The

Qur'anic text, however, distinguishes three groups: (i) believers (Muslims) (ii) unbelievers and polytheists, who are classed together as *mushriqs*, and (iii) People of the Book. Hypocrites are included within the group of Muslims since they were outwardly pretending to be believers even as they were inwardly defecting from Islam and scheming against the Muslims.

The Qur'an calls those who believe in the One God and the teachings of the Prophet Muhammed (pbuh) 'Muslims'. 'People of the Book' refers to those who follow a divine book and a prophet sent by God. While there is some difference of opinion on this, the general rule is that those who follow a book originally revealed by God are to be considered (and treated as) People of the Book even if their book has been changed and its teachings altered over the course of time. This definition includes Jews and Christians as well as others who believe in Abraham and David. The Qur'an counts the Sabians along with Jews and Christians in the following verses and therefore most exegetes and interpreters of the Qur'an (*mufassirs*) include them among the People of the Book:

> The [Muslim] believers, the Jews, the Christians, and the Sabians – those who believe in God and the Last Day and do good – will have their rewards with their Lord. No fear for them, nor will they grieve. (*al-Baqara*, 2:62)

> For the [Muslim] believers, the Jews, the Sabians, and the Christians – those who believe in God and the Last Day and do good deeds – there is no fear: they will not grieve. (*al-Ma'ida*, 5:69)

> As for the believers, those who follow the Jewish faith, the Sabians, the Christians, the Magians, and the idolaters, God will judge between them on the Day of Resurrection; God witnesses all things. (*al-Hajj*, 22:17)

According to some Islamic scholars, on the other hand, only Jews and Christians are People of the Book.[6]

More significantly, there are other scholars who argue that Jews and Christians are in fact *mushriq/kafir* based on the following verses:

---

6   Kamaluddin M. ibn al-Human, *Fath al-Qadir*, (Mısr, 1356/1937), vol.2, 372.

Those who say, 'God is the Messiah, son of Mary,' have defied
God... Those people who say that God is the third of three are
defying [the truth]: there is only One God. If they do not stop
what they are saying, a painful punishment will afflict those of
them who persist. (al-Ma'ida, 5:72–73)

There are some who insist that there are no real People of the Book today,
because idolatrous beliefs make Jews and Christians comparable to the
deniers of the One God, the *mushriqs*.[7] This forms the basis of their argument
against interfaith dialogue.

Hamdi Yazır of Elmalılı[8] provides the following explanation on the above
issue:

> *Mushriq* has two meanings in Qur'anic terminology: apparent
> and real. An apparent *mushriq* (polytheist or unbeliever) is
> one who openly believes in more than one God. Based on this
> meaning, People of the Book cannot be called *mushriqs* (i.e.
> polytheist or unbeliever). Real *mushriqs* are those who deny
> the oneness of God and Islam... Based on this meaning, Jews
> and Christians, who are People of the Book, are also *mushriqs*
> (polytheists or unbelievers).[9]

Said Nursi makes the following statement along the same lines:

> The word *kafir* (unbeliever) has two meanings: The first one
> that comes immediately to mind is 'unfaithful' and 'infidel' (one
> who denies the existence of God). We have no right to name the
> People of the Book (Jews and Christians) as such. The second
> meaning comprises those who deny our Prophet and Islam.
> Based on the latter meaning, we can name them as such and
> they will consent. However, because of the first meaning which
> is more common and comes first into mind, calling them *kafir*
> will be an insult and infliction.[10]

---

7   These people refer to beliefs such as the Christian claim that Jesus is the 'Son of God.'

8   Muhammed Hamdi Yazır Elmalılı (1878-1942) was a prominent Turkish Islamic scholar.

9   Muhammed Hamdi Yazır Elmalılı, *Hak Dini Kur'an Dili*, (İstanbul: Zehraveyn Yayınları, 1992), vol. 2, 221.

10 Bediüzzaman Said Nursi, *Münazarat*, (İstanbul: Yeni Asya Yayınevi, 1998), 71.

Those who claim that Jesus or Ezra was the 'Son' of God contradict the basic doctrine of the oneness of God, as strictly expounded in the Qur'an. Accordingly, from the point of view of credal doctrine, Christians, and the Jews mentioned in the Qur'an who considered Ezra as the 'Son' of God,[11] may be deemed *mushriqs*. However, the Qur'an still names and considers them 'People of the Book' so far as regulating Muslims' relations with them is concerned. Put differently, even if they are considered *mushriqs* in terms of credal confession, they are People of the Book by way of status in the Muslim society/polity. That is why (as we see below) the Qur'an calls upon Muslims to invite People of the Book to come to what is common between them, and to find common cause on that basis. Had Jews and Christians been *mushriqs* and nothing else the Qur'an would have presented them accordingly.

The key point here is that the Qur'an refers to Christians and Jews as 'People of the Book' even as it also acknowledges that they had departed from clear belief in the oneness of God and had altered their sacred scripture. For all that, the Muslims are called on to consider them as People of the Book and permitted, on that basis, to eat the animals they slaughtered and to marry women from among them. It follows that Muslims may call the present Jews and Christians 'People of the Book', since their beliefs are no more objectionable than those held by their ancestors at the time of the revelation of the Qur'an, who were treated as 'People of the Book.'[12]

On another note, we may make mention of a contemporary grouping among Jews or Christians who acknowledge that Muhammad (pbuh) was a true prophet, that Islam is a true religion and that the Qur'an is a divine revelation just like the Bible. When the Prophet (pbuh) performed the funeral prayer in absentia for the Abyssinian king Najashi, the *mushriqs* spread the rumour that 'he performed the funeral prayer for a Christian who died in Abyssinia,' upon which the following verse was revealed:

> Some of the People of the Book believe in God, in what has been sent down to you and in what was sent down to them: humbling themselves before God, they would never sell God's revelation for a small price. These people will have their rewards with their Lord: God is swift in reckoning. (al-'Imran, 3:199)

---

11   *Al-Tawba*, 9:23.

12   The Christian doctrine that Jesus is the 'Son of God' has not changed substantially since the time of the Prophet (pbuh). As to the belief in Ezra as 'Son of God', this belief is not held by contemporary Jews. (It is possible that it was restricted to a specific group at the time of the Prophet (pbuh).)

There are now considerable numbers of such people in the Western world, especially among scholarly circles, and they form a strong pillar of dialogue efforts between Muslims and the People of the Book, as noted by Bediüzzaman Said Nursi and Fethullah Gülen.[13]

Finally, we should remind ourselves that our interest here is not in how Islam categorises non-Muslims but rather in how it defines and regulates relationships with them. Since the Qur'an calls upon Muslims to engage in dialogue with People of the Book, among others, it is important for us to clarify who they are.

Attentiveness to the People of the Book should not be taken to be exclusive of others. The Qur'an also encourages dialogue with others, as we will see further below. At the time of revelation, the Qur'an particularly encouraged Muslims to engage in dialogue with those closest to them in belief, the People of the Book. This was, essentially, encouraging dialogue based on commonality. However, as we have shown from verses quoted earlier, the Qur'an also emphatically underlines our common humanity, our single ancestry, as the ground on which to base good relations, justice, respect and civility.[14] What is more our primary commonality is our humanity, and dialogue must be based on that single, fundamental truth: that we are the same. Whatever created one human being created the rest of humanity. Our source of creation and the innate disposition with which we have been created are one and the same.

Which verses command dialogue with People of the Book?

There are many verses in the Qur'an on the issue of dialogue with People of the Book:

> Say, 'People of the Book, let us arrive at a statement that is common to us all: we worship God alone, we ascribe no partner to Him, and none of us takes others beside God as lords.' (al-'Imran, 3:64)

Without doubt, this verse commands the Prophet (pbuh) and therefore the Muslims to establish relations with People of the Book and to unite around

---

13   Bediüzzaman Said Nursi, *Kaynaklı, İndeksli, Lügatlı Risale-i Nur Külliyatı*, (İstanbul: Nesil Basım Yayın, 1996), Vol. I, 663.
14   See 'What does the Qur'an say about dialogue?' above.

common issues. In a way, it draws a framework for dialogue. Common issues around which we can come together may be principles of faith such as faith in God, prophets and the afterlife, principles of practice such as abstinence from adultery, gambling or drinking, or temporal political, social, cultural or economic issues. The fact that the Prophet (pbuh) did not bring up points of conflict in his interactions with People of the Book, did not enter into combative debates with them and sought engagement with them through the Medina Charter and political and military treaties such as Hudaybiyya and Khaybar confirms that he carried out the Qur'anic command in letter and spirit.

Another verse mentions common points of faith and urges the avoidance of being disputatious and the building of positive, courteous relationship:

> [Believers], argue only in the best way with the People of the Book, except with those of them who act unjustly. Say, 'We believe in what was revealed to us and in what was revealed to you; our God and your God is one [and the same]; we are devoted to Him.' (al-'Ankabut, 29:46)

This verse also excepts those 'who act unjustly' from the norms of relationship commended generally. These are people who scarcely recognise the Muslims' right to exist as such and build their attitudes and relations with Muslim groups on the basis of permanent hostility. Whether this characterisation applies to an individual, a group or a state, Muslims are commanded to struggle against them within the laws and limits set by Islam. Indeed, it is not just a virtue but a religious duty (fard) to do so, according to the interpretations of scholars of Islamic law. However, any decision to strive to establish peace or pursue the option of war is a collective decision, not an individual one, and must be left to the relevant administrative and political authority. Individuals do not have the authority to start a war or to make peace.

Which verses command dialogue with non-Muslims generally?

The intelligibility of natural phenomena and the clear statements in the primary sources of Islam, especially when taken together, are strong evidence that God created in way that enables His creatures to know Him. But, for their part, they must strive to know Him, to be responsive to Him and to His creation. For humankind in particular, this striving takes the form of worship. The Qur'an makes this explicit in *al-Dhariyat*, 51:56:

> I created jinn and mankind only to worship Me.

It comes as no surprise, then, when we learn that we are commanded to be responsive not only to God and the phenomena of the world around us but also to other human beings. To engage in dialogue is essential to our God-given purpose and an integral element of the innate disposition (*fitra*) with which God has endowed human beings. How we should engage is indicated by the prophets that God inspired to communicate His will.

That God wills His creatures to engage respectfully and kindly with each other, in a dialogue parallel to their dialogue with Him, is shown by a number of verses in the Qur'an, including the following:

> And He does not forbid you to deal kindly and justly with anyone who has not fought you for your faith or driven you out of your homes: God loves the just. (*al-Mumtahana*, 60:8)

> People, We created you all from a single man and a single woman, and made you into races and tribes so that you should get to know one another. In God's eyes, the most honoured of you are the ones most mindful of Him: God is all knowing, all aware. (*al-Hujurat*, 49:13)

The non-Muslims mentioned in these verses clearly include any non-Muslims, not just People of the Book. The diversity among mankind mentioned in *al-Hujurat* 49:13 is mentioned with a comprehensive affirmation that its purpose is that different groups and individuals are thereby enabled to know each other. This point is underlined in several verses teaching that diversity in ethnicity, colour, faith and culture was intended by the Creator:

If God had so willed, He would have made you one community, but He wanted to test you through that which He has given you. (*al-Ma'ida*, 5:48)

If your Lord had pleased, He would have made all people a single community, but they continue to have their differences. (*Hud*, 11:118–19)

Had your Lord willed, all the people on earth would have believed. So can you [O Prophet] compel people to believe? (*Yunus*, 10:99)

Al-Hujurat, 49:13 encourages us to explore this diversity of ethnicity, culture and faith, engaging respectfully with different groups. The verses concerning difference of faith can be understood as encouraging Muslims (i) to accept that some individuals and groups will not believe in your faith however much you may desire them to; (ii) to live with the resulting differences in compassion and acceptance; (iii) to explore each other's faith and religion with respect and in an attempt to understand one another; (iv) to wait patiently until God explains what people have differed about and why.

The Qur'an's commanding or commending engagement with non-Muslims on the basis of justice, kindness, civility and courtesy, regardless of whether they are People of the Book, is embodied in the Prophetic Sunnah. The examples of the Prophet (pbuh) encourage Muslims to engage in peaceful relations and dialogue with other groups, not limited to Christians, Jews and Sabians. These examples will be explored further in a later chapter. Here it must suffice to remind readers of the shining example of the Medina Charter or Constitution, which the Prophet (pbuh) discussed, agreed and signed with the Jews and polytheists of Medina.

How should we understand the Qur'anic verses which seem to warn against trusting Jews and Christians?

There are several verses in the Qur'an which have meanings similar to that. For example:

> The believers should not make the unbelievers their allies rather than other believers – anyone who does such a thing will isolate himself completely from God – except when you need to protect yourselves from them. God warns you to beware of Him: the Final Return is to God. (al-'Imran, 3:28)

> You who believe, do not take the Jews and Christians as allies: they are allies only to each other. Anyone who takes them as an ally becomes one of them – God does not guide such wrongdoers. (al-Ma'ida, 5:51)

> The Jews and the Christians will never be pleased with you unless you follow their ways. Say, 'God's guidance is the only true guidance.' If you were to follow their desires after the knowledge that has come to you, you would find no one to protect you from God or help you. (al-Baqara, 2:120)

> You [Prophet] are sure to find that the most hostile to the believers are the Jews and those who associate other deities with God; you are sure to find that the closest in affection towards the believers are those who say, 'We are Christians,' for there are among them people devoted to learning and ascetics. (al-Ma'ida, 5:82)

> O you who believe! Do not take for intimate friends from among others than your own people; they do not fall short of inflicting loss upon you; they love what distresses you; vehement hatred has already appeared from out of their mouths, and what their breasts conceal is greater still; indeed, We have made the revelations clear to you, if you will understand. (al-'Imran, 3:118)

In order to understand these verses correctly, it is essential to ask which Jews and Christians are being referred to. The first step towards an answer is to consider the circumstances in which the verses were sent down, the occasions of their revelation (*asbab al-nuzul*). The decisive condition, it turns out, is being in a state of war or a state of peace.

For Muslims, peace is the default position. It is the most desirable state, to be welcomed wherever it is feasible, as evidenced in *al-Anfal*, 8:61:

> But if they incline towards peace, you [O Prophet] must also incline towards it, and put your trust in God: He is the All Hearing, the All Knowing.

The activity of peace-making is honoured and encouraged in verses such as *al-Baqara*, 2:224:

> [Believers], do not allow your oaths in God's name to hinder you from doing good, being mindful in everything of God and making peace between people. God hears and knows everything.

Peace is also portrayed as an essential element of the reward of those who obey God and adhere to the Qur'an, in this life and in the life to come:

> A light has now come to you from God, and a Scripture making things clear, with which God guides to the ways of peace those who follow what pleases Him, bringing them from darkness out into light, by His will, and guiding them to a straight path. (*al-Ma'ida*, 5:15–16)

> He is ever merciful towards the believers – When they meet Him, they will be greeted with 'Peace' – and He has prepared a generous reward for them. (*al-Ahzab*, 33:43–44)

All these verses underline the desirability of peace.

The example of the Prophet (pbuh) confirms that peace is the default Islamic position. His will for peace is clearly demonstrated by the Hudabiya pact. He chose to make a pact with the Meccans, rather than fight them, even though they had cruelly persecuted and driven away the Muslims, had tried to prevent them coming to worship in the city and demanded very unequal terms for any peace agreement.

The state of war is viewed as an exception but is recognised as unavoidable in some circumstances, that is, where there is active aggression from another group, when diplomacy has failed and the state declares war. Outside the exceptional circumstances of war, the default position, that is, peace, prevails. In these conditions Muslims are governed by those commands of the Qur'an and the Sunnah which regulate their conduct in the state of peace. Verses relating to war apply only in the exceptional state of war.

The verses here under discussion, forbidding friendship with Jews and Christians and warning against trusting them, fall into this category. All of the verses cited above were without doubt revealed in a war situation in which many Jews and Christians were de facto enemies engaged directly or indirectly in the effort to eliminate the Muslims. In other words, the verses concern the Jews and Christians who were active enemies of Muslims and made use of every opportunity to pursue that enmity.

Said Nursi comments on the scope of these verses as follows:

> The Qur'an's prohibition is not universal, it is absolute. And what is absolute can be defined within certain limits and conditions.[15]

That is to say, these verses, like the Qur'an in general, are always true and valid, but they are not necessarily relevant to our behaviour in every time and place. Just as the verses would have no immediate application to our conduct if we lived in an area where there were no Jews and Christians, they have no immediate application to our behaviour in a state of peace in relation to Jews and Christians who are not active enemies.

It is important also to note a key difference between the era of the Qur'an's revelation and our own. At the time of the revelation people's political allegiances were defined by their religion. Muslims were effectively 'citizens' of Islam, and Jews 'citizens' of a Jewish tribe, in the way that people today are citizens of a country such as the United Kingdom. When the Muslims were at war with local Jews it made sense to be wary because one would expect political loyalty to follow religious identity. In modern times political and religious allegiances are no longer so tightly bound together – people of different faiths are very often loyal to the same nation-state. Religious difference does not imply political enmity.

15   Nursi, *Münazarat*, 70.

Said Nursi makes a pertinent comment on another significant difference between the situation of the Prophet's (pbuh) time and our own. Not only are the political allegiances of modern Jews and Christians no longer generally tied to their religion; their identities and interests tend not to be so focused on faith. Some of their primary concerns may overlap with Muslims' concerns, and Muslims may be able to appreciate and learn from them on various levels:

> The Prophet's time was home to a major religious reform. Because all minds and attention were focused on religion, all love and hostility was related to religion. Therefore love for non-Muslims would be a sign of discord. But today's world is witnessing a curious civilisational reform. What occupies and intrigues all minds today is the level of civilisation and worldly advancement. Most of them are not so devoted to their religion anyway. We take them (non-Muslims) as friends to appreciate and adopt their civilisation and advancement; and to preserve law and order, which are the bases of all worldly happiness. This kind of friendship is certainly not prohibited by the Qur'an.[16]

Thus we see that on various levels the Jews and Christians that we are likely to encounter today may differ markedly from those who were the reason for the revelation of the verses in question. The verses do not regulate Muslim behaviour in a state of peace towards Jews and Christians who are not plotting against and attacking Muslims.

It is clear that even at the time of the revelation of these verses, those People of the Book who did not agree and co-operate with those of their co-religionists who had entered into a state of war against the Muslims would not be treated in the same way. The Qur'an makes it very explicit that, towards those non-Muslims who are not making war on the Muslims, the duties of justice, fairness, and kindness prevail:

> And He does not forbid you to deal kindly and justly with anyone who has not fought you for your faith or driven you out of your homes: God loves the just. (al-Mumtahana, 60:8)

Some of the People of the Book believe in God, in what has

---

16 Nursi, *Münazarat*, 70.

been sent down to you and in what was sent down to them: humbling themselves before God, they would never sell God's revelation for a small price. These people will have their rewards with their Lord: God is swift in reckoning. (al-'Imran, 3:199)

But they are not all alike. There are some among the People of the Book who are upright, who recite God's revelations during the night, who bow down in worship, who believe in God and the Last Day, who order what is right and forbid what is wrong, who are quick to do good deeds. These people are among the righteous and they will not be denied [the reward] for whatever good deeds they do: God knows exactly who is conscious of Him. (al-'Imran, 3:113–115)

The Prophet Muhammad's (pbuh) practice embodied the Qur'anic teaching. He did not treat all non-Muslims, or indeed all Jews, or all Christians, in the same way, indiscriminately, as if responding only to their being non-Muslims or to their particular confessional identity. When he signed a treaty with the Najran Christians, he was at war with the Meccan pagans at the same time. Similarly, when the Jews of Banu Qurayza were punished for violating the Medina Charter upon the judgement of the arbitrator whom they themselves had approved, he maintained the treaty with Banu Nadir, another Jewish tribe. He did not consider all the People of the Book as enemies. If he had done so his approval of practices such as marrying women from among them or sharing their food would be inexplicable. Rather, those social exchanges, alongside everyday commercial engagements, are a strong argument that for Muslims, the norms for how non-Muslims are regarded and treated do not derive from their values or their identity, but from their actions and how those actions are perceived in different political contexts. As Said Nursi has commented, 'If you had a wife from amongst the People of the Book, you would surely love her!'[17] meaning that a person's confessional identity does not, on its own, prevent a Muslim from befriending, or in the case of being married to them, loving that person from a different faith. He goes on to explain, 'Just as not all of the characteristics of an individual Muslim necessarily reflect the teachings of Islam, so also, not all of the qualities of followers of other religions are un-Islamic. That means that

---

17   Nursi, Münazarat, 70.

Islamic attributes and actions might easily be observed in non-Muslims.'[18]

In conclusion, the fact that a person was born to Jewish or Christian parents does not make him or her a relevant target of the Qur'anic verses cited at the beginning of this section. The grounds for the sort of relations advised by the verses in question are not religious; they are political. The application of these verses will depend on political conditions and political judgements, on whether, and to what extent, a particular group demonstrates hostility, and on whether or not they constitute a 'clear and present danger' in legal terms. According to Fethullah Gülen's interpretation, 'whether or not they turn religious beliefs or thoughts into a source and ground for active hostility' will play a key role in determining the appropriate approach to the group in question. Essentially, if and only if Jews or Christians have the same characteristics as the people who were the reason for the verses being revealed they will need to be regarded as 'enemies of the state'. It should be noted that only the state can declare any group 'enemies', just as only the state can declare war. Further, in accordance with the Sunnah as discussed above, those belonging to the faith of the 'enemy' group who do not behave as enemies should not be treated as such.

How should we understand verses in the Qur'an which command war against unbelievers?

Let us begin by first listing those verses that are often referred to when posing this question. They are:

1. Kill them wherever you encounter them, and drive them out from where they drove you out, for persecution (*fitna*) is more serious than killing. (*al-Baqara*, 2:191)

2. If they turn [on you], then seize and kill them wherever you encounter them. Take none of them as an ally or supporter. (*al-Nisa'*, 4:89)

3. When the [four] forbidden months are over, wherever you encounter the idolaters, kill them, seize them, besiege them, wait for them at every lookout post. (*al-Tawba*, 9:5)

---

18   Nursi, *Münazarat*, 70.

The issue of method mentioned in the previous question is again key to understanding correctly the messages that these verses give to the Muslims of the past, present and future. Proper methods of Qur'anic interpretation need to be followed in understanding individual verses as well as the whole of the Qur'an. Sound exegesis (*tafsir*) takes into account the demands of internal consistency in the Qur'an, the relevance of the occasions of revelation (*asbab al-nuzul*), and distinctions between the kinds of verses, for example between verses that are explicit and clearly understood (*muhkam*), or allegorical, whose referents are fully known only to God (*mutashabih*), or ambiguous in meaning (*mujmal*), or absolute (*mutlaq*) or restricted (*muqayyad*) in their entail for action, or abrogating (*nasikh*) or abrogated (*mansukh*).

The verses in question are frequently brought forth with no reference even to their immediate context, let alone their background, to say nothing of meeting the conditions of sound *tafsir* just mentioned. Such approaches suggest a biased attitude intended to prejudice any hope or possibility of allowing people to come together.

Having made these preliminary points, let us now look at the verses one by one.

1. Kill them wherever you encounter them (al-Baqara, 2:191)

This verse refers to the Meccan polytheists. In the period preceding the revelation of this verse, they did not recognise the Muslims' right to exist as such and drove them out of Mecca altogether, after persecuting and boycotting them as a group, and torturing and killing the weaker individuals among them, over a long period. Thereafter, in the Medina period, they violated the treaties they made with the Muslims. It was the Meccan polytheists who initiated hostilities and acts of war.

This verse was revealed after the Muslims had suffered nearly thirteen years of persecution at the Meccans' hands, after they had emigrated to Medina to escape persecution, after Meccan hostility persisted despite the Muslims' emigration and after the Meccans openly committed acts of war against the Muslims. In this situation, the Qur'an commanded:

> Fight in God's cause against those who fight you, but do not overstep the limits: God does not love those who overstep the limits. Kill them wherever you encounter them, and drive them

out from where they drove you out, for persecution is more serious than killing. Do not fight them at the Sacred Mosque unless they fight you there. If they do fight you, kill them – this is what such disbelievers deserve – but if they stop, then God is most forgiving and merciful. (*al-Baqara*, 2:190–192).

It is important to note that these three verses command fighting against those already engaged in war against the Muslims, but doing so in a restrained manner and observing the conventions about fighting in the sacred precincts of the Mosque, unless the enemy first breaches those conventions. We know from this and other verses that Muslims are also commanded to accept any offer of cease-fire from the opposite party at any stage of the war, and that Muslims should not be the party to start the war.[19]

2. ...seize and kill them wherever you encounter them. Take none of them as an ally or supporter (al-Nisa', 4:89)

The addressees of this verse are, notwithstanding the different opinions of some interpreters of the Qur'an, Meccan and Medinan hypocrites (*munafiqs*). Especially in the Medina period when the Muslims became a significant political power, certain individuals, groups and tribes who were not sincere Muslims began to behave in a way that constituted high treason. These hypocrites presented themselves as Muslims in the company of Muslims and as unbelievers when in the company of unbelievers. Because they were mixed in among the Muslims they posed an even more dangerous threat to them than did their declared enemies. According to one account they joined the Muslim forces for the Uhud war but later withdrew from the field, weakening and exposing those who remained. On this occasion the Muslims could not agree among themselves how to respond to this betrayal. However, in the following verse, God urged the believers not to get into a conflict because of the hypocrites:

> [Believers], why are you divided in two about the hypocrites, when God Himself has rejected them because of what they have done? Do you want to guide those God has left to stray? If God leaves anyone to stray, you [Prophet] will never find a way for him. (*al-Nisa'*, 4:88)

---

19   The exception is when war is the only feasible way of preventing oppression.

And He commanded the Muslims concerning what should be done:

> They would dearly like you to reject faith, as they themselves
> have done, to be like them. So do not take them as allies until
> they migrate [to Medina] for God's cause. If they turn [on you],
> then seize and kill them wherever you encounter them. Take
> none of them as an ally or supporter. (*al-Nisa*, 4:89)

When the verse is read in the context of the surrounding verses, and in its
historic context, its implications become much clearer.

Friend or confidant?

There are some who point to this same verse and argue that the Qur'an
prohibits Muslims from befriending non-Muslims. There are two points to
clarify here.

The first relates to the meaning of the word *wali* which has been translated
as 'friend' in some texts. Most exegetes (*mufassirs*) respected and accepted
by Muslims understand the word to mean in its context 'confidant' rather
than merely 'friend'. They explain that the verse advises against making
confidants of non-Muslims to the extent that you may disclose to them
what would nowadays be called 'state secrets'.[20] Isfahani, the author of *al-
Mufradat fi Gharib al-Qur'an*, supports this interpretation, saying that 'what
is prohibited is being subject to and being a confidant of'[21] non-Muslims.
This verse is reported to have been revealed in relation to a group of Muslims
who had intimate relations with the Jews in the pre-Islamic *Jahiliyya* period,
consulted them on all kinds of commercial or family issues and followed
their advice.[22] When it was suggested to 'Umar that he hire a young Christian
who had fine hand-writing as his clerk, he replied 'then I would be taking
him as a friend,' which shows that the verse can be interpreted as applying to
a relationship in which someone may have access to sensitive information.[23]
The prohibition includes not only unbelieving tribes but also any non-
Muslim relatives of a believer:

---

20   Abu al-Fida Ishmai'l ibn Kathir, *Tafsir al-Qur'an al-Azim*, (Beirut, 1961), vol.2, 342; Abu Ja'far Muhammad ibn Jarir
     al-Tabari, *Jami al-Bayan fi Ta'wil al-Qur'an*, (Cairo: Dar al-Maarif), vol.14, 175-176.

21   Al-Raghib al-Isfahani, *al-Mufradat fi Gharib al-Qur'an*, (İstanbul: Kahraman Yayınları, 1986), 837, 'Velayet' ('Confidants').

22   Al-Tabari, *Jami al-Bayan fi Ta'wil al-Qur'an*, vol.3, 406-407. Abu al-Fadl 'Abd al-Rahman ibn Abi Bakr Jalal al-Din
     al-Suyuti, *Asbab al-Nuzul*, (Cairo: Dar al-Manar), 43.

23   Orhan Atalay, *Doğu-Batı Kaynaklarında Birlikte Yaşama*, (İstanbul: Gazeteciler ve Yazarlar Vakfı Yayınları, 1999), 271.

> Believers, do not take your fathers and brothers as allies if they
> prefer disbelief to faith: those of you who do so are doing wrong.
> (*al-Tawba,* 9:23)

This further supports the argument that what is being prohibited is a
relationship that entails discussing secrets. This verse is not forbidding
Muslims to treat their non-Muslim relatives kindly; that would be against
the moral imperatives so clear from many verses of the Qur'an. What it is
saying is that in certain circumstances it would be a risk to share sensitive
information with them.

The second point that needs to be clarified is whether or not this prohibition
is qualified or absolute. To take an extreme example, given that Muslims
are permitted to marry Christian and Jewish women, is a Muslim man not
supposed to confide in his non-Muslim wife?

The prohibition of not taking a confidant again relates to the time of
war. This is clear from other verses in the Qur'an and from a holistic
understanding of the Qur'an as explained earlier, and also from historical
practice. Islamic history of all periods is full of instances of non-Muslims
holding senior positions in the state administration. During the Ottoman
period, for example, non-Muslims held ministerial positions in various state
departments including the Treasury, the Foreign Office, the Postal, Telegraph
and Telephone Department and the Ministry for the Imperial Treasury, as
well as serving as ambassadors and in the judiciary.[24] The Ottoman regime
recognised that the context for implementation of the verse *al-Nisa,* 4:89
was a state of war, and that the verse was not intended to regulate their
behaviour in a state of peace. Similarly, Muslims living in a plural society in
a state of peace are by no means forbidden to befriend non-Muslims. Nor
are Muslim men who marry non-Muslims required to withhold confidences
from them.

---

24 To give just a few examples, Alexander Karatheodori Pasha was the Head Commissioner of the Porte to the Congress of Berlin
of 1878. Agop Kazazyan Pasha (1880–1891) and Sakız Ohannes Pasha (1897-1908) served as Ministers for Finance and for
the Imperial Treasury respectively, while Gabriel Noradunkyan Efendi (1912-13) served as Foreign Minister. (See 'Armenians
in Ottoman Bureaucracy' article on the Republic of Turkey's Ministry for Foreign Affairs website, accessed 6th October 2011,
http://www.mfa.gov.tr/armenians-in-ottoman-bureaucracy.en.mfa .)

Different responses to different polytheist attitudes

The verse in question (*al-Nisa'*, 4:89)[25] was originally revealed in relation to hypocritical Meccan polytheists. From the very beginning they opposed and oppressed the Muslims, never fully complied with the peace treaties they signed and sought every opportunity to manipulate the terms to harass and defeat the Prophet (pbuh). As is made clear in the following verse 90, those polytheists who wish to live in peace and honour the terms of the treaty are exempted from the preceding verse. Put differently, verse 89 is not about Meccan polytheists as a whole but only about those of them who violated the peace treaty by fighting against the Muslims. Verse 91 explains that Muslims are permitted to kill the polytheists only if they actively pursue hostilities towards the Muslims and war breaks out:

> You will find others who wish to be safe from you, and from their own people, but whenever they are back in a situation where they are tempted [to fight you], they succumb to it. So if they neither withdraw, nor offer you peace, nor restrain themselves from fighting you, seize them and kill them wherever you encounter them: We give you clear authority against such people. (*al-Nisa'*, 4:91)

The default position is peace. By this we mean that unless there is active hostility and war, the verses in the Qur'an that relate to war are not applicable. In a state of peace, the Qur'an does not permit, still less encourage, the killing of other people. Where there is dispute it urges and requires diplomacy. And there can be no bloodshed during a diplomatic negotiation. But if that fails and the state declares war, then Muslims are permitted to engage the enemy during war. The enemy is defined very strictly, and those who no longer wish to fight, or who are covered by the protection of any treaty, are not to be fought:

> But as for those who reach people with whom you have a treaty, or who come over to you because their hearts shrink from fighting against you or against their own people, God could have given them power over you, and they would have fought you. So if they withdraw and do not fight you, and offer you peace, then God gives you no way against them.
> (*al-Nisa'*, 4:90)

---

25 'If they turn [on you], then seize and kill them wherever you encounter them. Take none of them as an ally or supporter.' (*al-Nisa'*, 4:89.)

3. When the [four] forbidden months are over, wherever you encounter the idolaters, kill them, seize them, besiege them, wait for them at every lookout post (al-Tawba, 9:5)

The final verse concerns the polytheists who violate treaties. The context and background given in the Qur'an itself make it clear without any need for interpretation:

> A release by God and His Messenger from the treaty you [believers] made with the idolaters [is announced] – you [idolaters] may move freely about the land for four months, but you should bear in mind both that you will not escape God, and that God will disgrace those who defy [Him]. On the Day of the Great Pilgrimage [there will be] a proclamation from God and His Messenger to all people: 'God and His Messenger are released from [treaty] obligations to the idolaters. It will be better for you [idolaters] if you repent; know that you cannot escape God if you turn away.' As for those idolaters who have honoured the treaty you [believers] made with them and who have not supported anyone against you: fulfil your agreement with them to the end of their term. God loves those who are mindful of Him. (al-Tawba, 9:1–4)

By contrast, for those who violate the treaty terms:

> When the [four] forbidden months are over, wherever you encounter the idolaters, kill them, seize them, besiege them, wait for them at every lookout post; but if they repent, maintain the prayer, and pay the prescribed alms, let them go on their way, for God is most forgiving and merciful. If any one of the idolaters should seek your protection [Prophet], grant it to him so that he may hear the word of God, then take him to a place safe for him, for they are people who do not know. How could there be a treaty with God and His Messenger for idolaters? – But as for those with whom you made a treaty at the Sacred Mosque, so long as they remain true to you, be true to them; God loves those who are mindful of Him. (al-Tawba, 9:5-7)

It was a local custom to refrain from fighting during the sacred months in pre-Islamic Arab culture. The Qur'an urges Muslims to respect that custom and avoid fighting during those months. 'Then slay them wherever you find them,' relates to a state of war. If war continues after a sacred month, Muslims are permitted to engage the enemy. They are permitted to kill those that attempt to kill them. However, if the 'enemy' drops his weapon and asks for peace, even during battle, then the Qur'an requires Muslims to seek peace.

But who are the idolaters that the Qur'an is addressing in this verse? It describes them by highlighting their attitudes and behaviour towards the Muslims as follows:

> [How,] when, if they were to get the upper hand over you, they would not respect any tie with you, of kinship or of treaty? They please you with their tongues, but their hearts are against you and most of them are lawbreakers. They have sold God's message for a trifling gain, and barred others from His path. How evil their actions are! Where believers are concerned, they respect no tie of kinship or treaty. They are the ones who are committing aggression. If they repent, keep up the prayer, and pay the prescribed alms, then they are your brothers in faith: We make the messages clear for people who understand. But if they break their oath after having made an agreement with you and revile your religion, then fight these leaders of disbelief – oaths mean nothing to them – so that they may stop. (al-Tawba, 9:8–12)

They are, in essence, people who cannot be trusted to respect the terms of treaties; indeed, they 'break their oath after having made an agreement.' They are thus a constant threat to the lives of the Muslims who have tried to establish peace with them through such treaties.

After all this explanation, the Qur'an addresses the Muslims to encourage and motivate them in the war they must fight:

> How could you not fight a people who have broken their oaths, who tried to drive the Messenger out, who attacked you first? Do you fear them? It is God you should fear if you are true

believers. Fight them: God will punish them at your hands, He will disgrace them, He will help you to conquer them, He will heal the believers' feelings and remove the rage from their hearts. God turns to whoever He wills in His mercy; God is all knowing and wise. (*al-Tawba*, 9:13–15)

Conclusions

Taking all these Qur'anic passages together we can make a number of observations.

Firstly, Muslims are not asked to treat all members of the other party in one and the same way, even if they are hypocrites or idolaters. We are asked to treat differently those who are actively hostile towards the Muslims, those who ask for protection from the Muslims, and those who remain neutral.

Secondly, the command to 'kill' appears in only three passages in the Qur'an. Central in each of them is the issue of being 'true to one's covenant'. As the three passages record, the idolaters and hypocrites broke their treaties with the Prophet (pbuh) at various times. According to the customs of the time, breaking a peace treaty, which inevitably threatens the security of the other signatories, was a cause of war. The Qur'an takes this line. The hypocrites made secret agreements and co-operated with the idolaters against the Muslims and thereby violated their obligations under the treaties.

Thirdly, the command to kill, which occurs in the three Qur'anic passages cited and discussed above, relates to the political decision that is appropriate when one is being persecuted and fought by a persistent enemy. Muslims were not permitted to wage war or retaliate for thirteen years while they were persecuted and killed at the hands of the Meccans. They migrated to Medina but still the persecution and hostility continued. Covenants were made and then broken by the Meccans. Only at this point did the Qur'an permit the Muslims to engage in war to defend themselves against this ongoing aggression.

Therefore, the commands to kill that we have discussed pertain to particular political situations and are not universal religious values. This is not to say that religious values do not or should not incorporate practical politics and legal realities. Rather, we need to distinguish between, on the one hand, a *de facto* reality and the response proper to it and, on the other, universal values.

Surat al-Tawba makes reference to a particular and exceptional basis for war.[26] The command to be vigilant against the idolaters, capture them, and if necessary kill them, instructed believers to take the measures necessary to rescue the Ka'ba from the presence and dominion of the idolaters.[27]

Yet, even then, the Qur'an consistently stipulates that the other party has to violate a treaty or start a war in order for Muslims to execute the command to kill, that a cease-fire should be made immediately when the other party makes a request and that Muslims must give protection to those who ask for it. This shows us very clearly what the underlying universal values are: evidently, even the regulations governing a state of war and military operations are heavily weighted towards tolerance.

The declaration of war is another issue highlighted in the Qur'an that needs to be dwelt upon. The need to declare the termination of an existing treaty and the start of hostilities had never been underlined to this extent in any other legal system before.

Reviewing the rules of active war as set forth by scholars of Islamic law will provide a final overview of the issue in its entirety:

1. The war must be declared by the state. The war must end when the opposing party asks for protection. (*al-Tawba*, 9:6)

2. Distinctions must be made between enemy combatants and non-combatants. The clergy, civilians, children and women serving behind the fronts must not be touched. (The Prophet's (pbuh) response upon seeing a woman killed on the battlefield underlines this. He said: 'But she was not fighting.')[28]

---

26 'When the forbidden months are over, wherever you encounter the idolaters, kill them, seize them, besiege them, wait for them at every lookout post... How could you not fight a people who have broken their oaths, who tried to drive the Messenger out, who attacked you first?... It is not right for the idolaters to tend God's places of worship while testifying to their own disbelief...' (*al-Tawba*, 9:5, 13, 17.)

27 Committee appointed by Turkey's National Directorate of Religious Affairs (Diyanet), *Kur'an Yolu*, (Ankara: Diyanet İşleri Başkanlığı Yayınları, 2003), vol. 3, 12-13.

28 Muhammed b. Ahmad Sarahsi, *Sherh al-Siyar al-Kabeer*, (Beirut, 1997), vol. 1, 32.

3. The enemy must do actual harm. Accordingly, those who have not caused actual damage cannot be killed on the battlefield even if they are combatants.[29] They can only be captured and then must be humanely treated during their captivity. The Prophet (pbuh), who did not curse even those of his enemies who had tried to kill him in battle, sets a great example in this regard.[30]

4. Although it was widely practised in the *Jahiliyya* (pre-Islamic) period and was still applied to the Muslim martyrs by their enemies, Muslims were forbidden to mutilate the bodies of those killed in battle.[31] The Prophet (pbuh), who valued people for their humanity, even forbade speaking negatively of dead enemies and took great care not to offend their living relatives.[32]

In short, peace is Islam's essential and default position. War is a temporary situation and is defined as the occurrence of a military clash due to political conflicts.[33] Religious difference can never be in itself a cause of war (*casus belli*). On the basis of the Qur'an and Sunnah, most Islamic scholars have agreed that war can be legitimately waged in self-defence or to prevent oppression. And even killing during warfare is regulated by rules. Such rules were set forth by the Qur'an and the Prophet (pbuh), were followed to the letter by the first caliphs and were recorded as principles of war in books of Islamic jurisprudence.[34] The verses commanding absolute war mentioned in the question concern situations in which peace-making through diplomacy has become impossible.

---

29   Burhanuddin Merginani, *Al-Hidaya Sharhu Bidayati'l-Mubtadi*, (İstanbul: 1986).

30   Sarahsi, *Sherh al-Siyar al-Kabeer*, vol. 1, 56.

31   Muhammad ibn Isma'il al-Bukhari, *Sahih al-Bukhari*, Maghazi, hadith no. 36.

32   Muhammad b. 'Isa al Tirmidhi, *Jami al-Tirmidhi*, Birr, hadith no. 51.

33   Ali Bulaç, 'Cihat,' *Yeni Ümit*, 63(2004): 48.

34   Güneş, Ahmet, 'Views on the Rules of the War,' in *Terror and Suicide Attacks: an Islamic Perspective*, ed. Ergun Çapan, (New Jersey: The Light Inc, 2004), 127-8.

Is the legal maxim *pacta sunt servanda* (agreements must be kept) binding in relations with non-Muslims?

It is important for our topic to discuss the political, military and legal aspects of this principle within the framework of the treaties that Muslims made with non-Muslims at the time of the revelation of the Qur'an.

According to the Qur'an and the Sunnah, treaties cannot be terminated unilaterally at the discretion of either party and they are binding on the signatories in all respects. They derive their sanction not only from the wording of their text but also from general religious and moral principles. That is why the principle that 'agreements must be kept' is stressed in the Sunnah and Islamic sources.

The Qur'an underlines the significance of abiding by agreements, keeping one's word at all times and mutual trust, by reminding people that they are accountable to God for their conduct relating to an agreement:

> Fulfil any pledge you make in God's name and do not break oaths after you have sworn them, for you have made God your surety: God knows everything you do. Do not use your oaths to deceive each other – like a woman who unravels the thread she has firmly spun – just because one party may be more numerous than another. God tests you with this, and on the Day of the Resurrection He will make clear to you those things you differed about. (*al-Nahl,* 16:91-92)

The metaphor for unilaterally violating an agreement is striking. Sayyid Qutb explains this as follows:

> A person who goes back on his pledges is shown like a stupid, imbecile woman who has no resolve. She spins her yarn and then breaks it, leaving it in loose thread. Every little detail given in the example suggests shame and ignominy. The whole picture is meant to give a completely repulsive impression. No honourable person would compromise himself to look so idiotic as the woman who spends her life doing what is of no use and no value whatsoever.[35]

---

35   Sayyid Qutb, *In the Shade of the Qur'an, Fi Zilal al Qur'an,* trans. and ed. Abil Salahi, (Markfield: The Islamic Foundation, 2001), vol. 11, 89, *al-Nahl,* 16:92.

The Qur'an draws particular attention to the superiority of one party over another in terms of manpower and ammunition as a reason for unilateral violation of treaties '...because one party may be more numerous than another ...'[36] One of the main reasons for people breaking their word is that they think they have the power to get away with it. Such treachery in the name of 'the national interest', of which we see countless examples, especially in the modern world, is against Islamic morality.

The Prophet (pbuh) likewise forbade breaking one's word. This prohibition applies to private individuals and to public authorities. He also prohibited violating treaties, plotting against the other party and raiding them. The Prophetic *hadith* (saying) 'The best among you are those who abide by the terms of agreements,'[37] encapsulates his teaching.

It is striking that respecting agreements is such a fundamental principle in the Qur'an that Muslims must reject any requests from fellow Muslims for help in a conflict against a non-Muslim party if they have signed a treaty with that party. The Qur'an refers to this principle as follows:

> Those who believed and emigrated [to Medina] and struggled for God's cause with their possessions and persons, and those who gave refuge and help, are all allies of one another. As for those who believed but did not emigrate, you are not responsible for their protection until they have done so. But if they seek help from you against religious persecution, it is your duty to help them, except against people with whom you have a treaty: God sees all that you do. (*al-Anfal,* 8:72)

This shows that respecting treaty obligations is considered a sacred duty and given priority even over Islamic brotherhood and the duty to secure fellow Muslims against persecution.

It is absolutely clear from relevant verses in the Qur'an that respecting agreements is just as important for Muslims when they make agreements with non-Muslims as when they make agreements with other Muslims. In either case, Islamic teaching holds that there can be no excuse for violating agreements.

---

36 *Al-Nahl*, 16:92.

37 Ahmad b. 'Ali b. al-Muthanna Abu Ya'la al-Mawsili, *Musnad*, vol.2, 318.

'And fight them until there is no more persecution (fitna)...' (al-Baqara, 2:193). Does this verse not see unbelief as a casus belli?

Some scholars, having interpreted the word '*fitna*' in this verse as 'associating partners with God', argue that this and similar verses[38] which command war with people of other faiths cancel all other verses that command peace.[39]

However, we can see the error of this interpretation by considering the use of '*fitna*' elsewhere in the Qur'an. It occurs 34 times altogether and its derivatives are used 26 times. It means trial, oppression, persecution and torture, disaster, misguidance, madness, suffering, sin, war and turmoil depending on the context in which it is used.[40] It should be noted that 'associating partners with God' is not among those meanings and nowhere in the Qur'an has the word '*fitna*' been used to convey that meaning. On the other hand, there is no doubt that forcing people to convert, violating God's prohibitions, creating disorder and sending people into exile are considered *fitna*.

Fitna in this verse is best interpreted as applying to the persecution of Muslims to force their conversion from Islam. The occasion of its revelation points in this direction. Meccan idolaters tortured some Muslims in the sacred months and killed them. The verse tells Muslims that responding to such mistreatment is more important than respecting the sacred months and permits them to fight to stop such persecution.[41] Therefore the common interpretation of most scholars is that stopping *fitna* in this verse means stopping or preventing the forced conversion of Muslims and the threat of a collective attack from the enemy; and sustaining an environment of freedom of religion.[42] The suppression of religious freedom is an act of oppression which can legitimately be dealt with by armed struggle if it cannot be prevented by other means. However, fighting for the right to practice and

38   Such as *al-Tawba*, 9:15.

39   Haşim Cemil, 'al-Salaam fi al-Islam,' *Risala al-Islamiyya* 63-64: 43.

40   Muhammad ibn Mukarram ibn Ali ibn Ahmad ibn Manzur, *Lisan al-Arab*, (Beirut: Dar Sadr), vol.13, 317-320; Abu al-Tahir ibn Ibrahim Majd al-Din al-Fairuzabadi, *Al-Qamus al-Muhit*, 1575; Abu al-Fadl 'Abd al-Rahman ibn Abi Bakr Jalal al-Din al-Suyuti, *Al-Itqan fi 'Ulum al-Qur'an*, (Cairo: Halabi, 1354/1935), vol. 1, 186; Muhammad Mahzun, *Tahqiq Mawaqif al-Sahaba fi al-Fitna: min Riwayat al-Iman al-Tabari wa al-Muhaddithin*, (Riyadh, 1994), vol. 1, 267ff; Mesut Erdal, 'Kur'an'da Fitne Kavramı Üzerine Düşünceler,' *DUIFD* 1(1991): 221. See also Muhammad Fuad Abdul Baqi, *Al Mujam el Mofahras Li Alfaz al Qur'an al Kareem*, (Damascus: Dar al Hadeeth), 511-2.

41   Suat Yıldırım, *Kuran-ı Hakim ve Açıklamalı Meali*, (İstanbul: Define Yayınları, 1998), 29.

42   Committee appointed by Turkey's National Directorate of Religious Affairs (Diyanet), *Kur'an Yolu*, vol. 1, 199.

preach the religion of one's choice is an entirely different matter to fighting in order to propagate that religion, which cannot be a cause of war according to Islamic principles.

Taking unbelief as a *casus belli* would mean forcing everyone to convert to Islam or otherwise killing them. Most people from the West who think of Islam as a 'religion of the sword' have this kind of approach in mind. However, extensive evidence demonstrates that the verse in question does not mean that unbelief is a *casus belli*. The verse itself continues as follows: 'If they cease hostilities, there can be no further hostility, except towards aggressors.' This tells us that the verse is concerned about objectionable hostile actions, not a state of belief or unbelief. Numerous verses in the Qur'an teach that faith is a matter of personal choice. The Qur'an also teaches that Muslims are responsible only for explaining their religion (*al-Kahf*, 18:29, *al-Hujurat*, 49:14); they are not commanded to force it on others. The Prophet's (pbuh) practice entirely supports this position; numerous examples include the Medina Charter, the Hudaybiyya pact and the amnesty after the conquest of Mecca.[43] Finally there are the scores of verses commanding or commending peace and tolerance, such as 'deal kindly and justly with anyone who has not fought you for your faith,' (*al-Mumtahana*, 60:8), 'There is no compulsion in religion,' (*al-Baqara*, 2:256), and 'Do not let your hatred for the people who barred you from the Sacred Mosque induce you to break the law,' (*al-Ma'ida*, 5:2), which unambiguously oppose the notion that unbelief can be a valid *casus belli*.

From a Qur'anic perspective, is relationship with non-Muslims normally based on war or peace?

What is fundamental and the default position in the religious teaching of Islam is not war but peace, tolerance, forgiveness and love. War is nevertheless a lawful means that may be resorted to when it is absolutely necessary and unavoidable. Islamic scholars have generally agreed that, according to the principles and examples of the Qur'an and Sunnah, war is justified in self-defence or to prevent oppression. Enemy actions against Muslims' security of property, religion, homeland and life, violation of treaties, attacks and persecution, are, accordingly, legitimate causes of war.[44] The verse 'Fight in

---

43   Abu Dawud al-Sijistani, *Sunan Abu Dawud*, Jihad, 121.

44   War can only be declared by the state.

God's cause against those who fight you, but do not overstep the limits' (*al-Baqara*, 2:190) sums up this position.

Not transgressing the limits is the basic principle of war.

> You who believe, be steadfast in your devotion to God and bear witness impartially: do not let hatred of others[45] lead you away from justice, but adhere to justice, for that is closer to awareness of God. Be mindful of God: God is well aware of what you do. (*al-Ma'ida*, 5:8)

Fakhr al-Din al-Razi states that the scope of this verse is universal. It commands Muslims to treat justly even those who exceed the limits in doing evil and it forbids persecution and injustice.[46]

Commanding the good (*amr bi-l-ma'ruf*), preaching and advising (*wa'z* and *nasiha*) and speaking mild words (*al-qawl al-layyin*) are not only principles of communicating Islam, they also reflect the basic moral code of Muslims. The prophets who are mentioned and whose lives are presented as examples in the Qur'an are held responsible for communicating the divine truth with civility but not for making people believe (e.g. *Yunus*, 10:99; *Saba'*, 34:27). The Qur'an emphasises that persuading people through reason is the key (*al-'Ankabut*, 29:61) and that the prophets and messengers did not quit the path of benevolence and tolerance despite the insults, persecutions and tortures inflicted on them by the people they were trying to help; Moses, for example, was commanded to speak gently even to the Pharaoh (*Ta-Ha*, 20:44). All of these events narrated by the Qur'an emphasise peace, love, tolerance and forgiveness rather than war.

When we look at the Prophet's (pbuh) life from this perspective, we do not see a different picture. At the conquest of Mecca he forgave those people who subjected him and the believers to persecution and war over the course of two decades, and he refrained from the usual practices of taking booty and prisoners. Like Joseph to his brothers, he said to the Meccan idolaters who were expecting execution: 'This day let no reproach be cast on you! You are all free.'[47]

---

45   This resumes the instruction in vv.1-2.

46   Fakhr al-Din al-Razi, *Al-Tafsir al-Kabir*, (Beirut: Dar Ihya al-Turath al'Arabi), vol. 3, 560.

47   Abu Muhammad 'Abd al-Malik ibn Hisham, *As-Sirah an-Nabawiyyah*, vol.2, 274

Do the verses on war in the Qur'an abrogate the verses on peace?

The verses in the Qur'an urging the believers to fight and those urging them to peace each have their particular rationale, as their occasions of revelation clearly show. The fact that the Prophet (pbuh) concluded a peace treaty with the idolaters on one front while fighting a different group of idolaters on another makes the point. Similarly, the Prophet (pbuh) maintained peaceful relations with one Jewish tribe while he punished another Jewish tribe who broke their agreement and fought against the believers. Such cases demonstrate that the verses commanding the believers to fight regulate conduct towards other groups only in particular circumstances. Therefore the interpretation that the verses on war override those on peace is not correct. The gradual development of the provisions on war might give credit to such an interpretation but an integrated approach to the teaching of the Qur'an and Sunnah invalidates it.

We must recognise nevertheless that, over the course of time, it proved difficult to sustain the balanced teaching on war and peace, which favours the latter unless conditions forbid it. Different schools of Islamic law (*madhhabs*), which have divergent rulings on many issues, are generally in agreement on issues related to war. Generally, but not always. For example, the Hanafis do not think that unbelief constitutes a *casus belli* whereas the Shafi'is do. For the most part, though, the legal schools settled on interpretations sanctioning war that do not hold the balance favoured in the Qur'an and the Prophet's (pbuh) example. These later interpretations were no doubt strongly influenced by the conditions of ongoing hostilities during which they were written down. It would be easy for scholars, living through such conditions, to overstate the area of implementation of the Qur'anic verses on war because of the sheer imminence of war in the general consciousness at the time, and, in doing so, to understate the duty to build and sustain peaceful relations.

Jurisprudence on *jihad* reached a settled formulation at the beginning of the Abbasid period. It could be argued that, given the considerable empire and military might that the Abbasids took over from the Umayyads, they did not feel any great need to develop a doctrine of active peaceful engagement with non-Muslim peoples. In fact, the Abbasids pursued what would nowadays be called a 'realistic' policy, making alliances with the Franks, for example, against the Umayyads still in power in Spain. It is at least conceivable that the scholars found themselves emphasising the 'duty' of war against non-Muslims in order to dissuade the Muslims from making war among themselves.

While we might expect that this emphasis should have encouraged the Muslims to build up negative attitudes to non-Muslim 'others', this did not happen. The period of Abbasid rule, when the jurisprudence on *jihad* was written down, is the period when it became almost a state policy to recognise virtue and knowledge in the cultures and traditions of non-Muslims within and beyond the boundaries of the Islamic empire. Aside from the benefits that accrued from this policy in travel information, trade and material prosperity, there were the cultural benefits that led to and grew out of the so-called 'translation movement'. The project of gathering and translating the great works of philosophy and natural sciences from the ancient world, west and east, required Muslims and non-Muslims to share intellectual space across cultural and linguistic barriers, to agree common standards of argumentation and expression and the habits of civility that make dialogue possible and beneficial.

In sum, even (what we consider to be) the later overemphasis on the Qur'anic verses authorising war, at the expense of the verses urging peace, did not produce in the Muslims generally the kind of hateful attitudes to non-Muslims that would exclude dialogue or peaceful relations. Muslims themselves naturally attribute this to the fundamental spirituality, sanity and balance that characterise the message of the Qur'an and its practical embodiment in the Sunnah. The claim that the verses on war abrogate the verses on peace simply does not hold.

Are 'jihad' and 'dialogue' not contradictory concepts?

The idea that '*jihad*' and 'dialogue' are contradictory concepts is based on an erroneous understanding of *jihad*. If *jihad* is conceived as indiscriminate armed struggle against non-Muslims, or as the expansion of an Islamic state through military conquest, then of course it is in contradiction with the respectful engagement of dialogue. However, those are gross misconceptions of *jihad*, which need to be corrected.

Jihad has been greatly misunderstood by both Muslims and non-Muslims. Muslims have sometimes even called the civil wars among themselves '*jihad*'; on the other side, non-Muslims describe terrorist attacks as 'holy war' or 'Islamic *jihad*' based on the religious background and claims of the terrorists. Since it is an Islamic concept that is constantly disputed, its meaning should be settled by reference to the indisputably authoritative framework of the Qur'an and the Prophet's (pbuh) practice, his Sunnah. Going beyond this framework risks distorting the structure in which the concept fits and operates.

Let us briefly consider the sources of the various misunderstandings of *jihad* before we endeavour to correct those misunderstandings. On the non-Muslim side, the concept of *jihad* has long been distorted by many poorly informed writers on Islam. Since at least the time of the Western Orientalists, who studied 'the East' in earnest during the colonialist nineteenth century, there have been plenty of outsiders who have misunderstood and misrepresented the *jihad* concept. Authors whose sources of information were very limited and whose observations were manifestly coloured by prejudice exercised a wide influence among severely under-informed Westerners. There have been numerous negative representations of *jihad* on the lines of 'religious expansionism that threatens civilisation,' 'terrorism or blind fanaticism for a political cause,' or 'fanaticism fuelled by religious ignorance.' Even those who should or could have known better have often more or less followed this approach.

For example, one of the most influential Orientalists of the twentieth century, Joseph Schacht, appears to understand *jihad* in expansionist terms:

> The basis of the Islamic attitude towards unbelievers is the law
> of war; they must be either converted or subjugated or killed
> (excepting women, children and slaves).[48]

Muslims too have developed distorted ideas of *jihad*. The twentieth century was marked by the shadow of Western colonialism, of which the Muslim world suffered its share. In order to struggle against colonialism and its worst effects, some Muslims organised armed or unarmed resistance movements. The notion of *jihad* served as a powerful tool for such organisations and

---

48   Joseph Schacht, *An Introduction to Islamic Law*, (Oxford: Oxford University Press, 1964), 130.

the religious scholars who functioned as their theoreticians. *Jihad* became a motivating factor in the struggle for the preservation of the five basic rights and moral values[49] against the Western invasion. In this struggle the methods used included armed defence. Against this background the word *jihad* came to be known only through its 'war' meaning, its other meanings being set aside.

In addition, the wars fought, during the period of the Prophet (pbuh), the Four Righteous Caliphs and their successors, against the idolaters, Christians and Jews tended to be mistakenly perceived, interpreted and named as religious wars.[50] This understanding and the resistance against colonial rule caused a shift in the meaning of *jihad* within the Islamic tradition and put its war aspect in the forefront.

In our times, misconceptions of *jihad* have been exacerbated by those who have claimed to be engaging in *jihad* while committing acts of terrorism against civilians. Although such acts are completely at odds with Islam's basic principles, the claims of their perpetrators have led many ill-informed Westerners to understand *jihad* as encompassing indiscriminate acts of violence in the name of Islam. Many non-Muslims have made the mistake of on the one hand condemning the terrorists in the strongest terms while on the other hand failing to question their interpretation of religious concepts. Coming after centuries of misrepresentation of *jihad*, the impression made in the West by al-Qaeda-style terrorism has led to new extremes of misunderstanding. For example, the American Wesleyan pastor James L. Garlow writes:

> There is an 'unofficial' sixth pillar of Islam, particularly of fundamentalist Muslims: jihad. The term 'jihad' means 'struggle' and can mean something as innocuous as the personal internal struggle to obey God or the struggle against the devil. Unfortunately, it can be something as violent as killing those who do not believe in Islam. Jihad has four potential expressions... It

---

49   *Jihad* in the sense of armed struggle has its place in Muslim conduct when one needs to use force to protect one's faith, person, family, property and land from attack and the state has declared war.

50   These wars were not, in fact, caused by or justified by religious differences. The wars fought under the Prophet (pbuh) and the Four Righteous Caliphs were fought in legitimate defence of persons, religious freedom, property or land or when other parties wilfully broke treaties. Later wars may not always have adhered to the stringent principles of war given in the Qur'an and the Sunnah, but where they departed from these norms they were fundamentally fought for political reasons, not religious ones. For further discussion of this issue please see the introductory section of Chapter 4, 'The Historical Basis'.

is the fourth use of the term 'jihad' that highlights the violent component of Islam. Jihad of the sword: defending Islam and, as many persons have come to experience in Muslim countries, attacking in the name of Allah – including such things as kidnappings and bombings.[51]

Having briefly examined some of the sources of the distortion of the concept, we can now try to clarify its true Islamic meaning. *Jihad* is derived from the root *j–h–d* and refers to 'making effort, using all possible means to achieve something.'[52] In Islamic literature, it has been defined as 'learning, teaching and implementing religious commands, commanding good and forbidding evil, struggling against the ego's desires,' and as a term of *fiqh* (Islamic jurisprudence) it means 'armed and unarmed struggle against external enemies.'[53] It has also been defined as 'working in the path of God with one's body, property, tongue, pen and all other means,'[54] 'making every possible effort to reach a goal,'[55] 'all types of activities and efforts to teach the religion of God,'[56] 'struggling to gain freedom both in one's inner and outer world,'[57] and 'making effort to remove obstacles between people and God.' It is the balance of internal and external conquest. *Jihad* is a comprehensive notion and its content changes according to the conditions of the time. Since *jihad* means endeavour for the sake of God, it of course includes armed struggle to protect one's faith, person, family, property and land against aggressors when the state has declared war. But engaging in physical armed defence is only one of the many meanings and daily manifestations of *jihad*. The majority of Muslims engage in non-armed *jihad* in their lives. As such, defining *jihad* as synonymous with 'holy war' is both linguistically, Islamically, and by way of practice, very wrong and unhelpful.[58]

As understood from the above definitions, *jihad* has two dimensions; one is physical effort and endeavour (which can include but is certainly not

51   James Garlow, *A Christian's Response to Islam*, (Oklahoma: River Oak Publishing, 2002), 44.

52   Ibn Manzur, *Lisan al-Arab*, vol.3, 133, 'j.h.d.'

53   Abu Bakr al-Jassas al-Razi, *Ahkam al-Qur'an*, vol.3, 208; Ahmet Özel, 'Cihat,' in *DİA (Diyanet İslam Ansiklopedisi)*, (İstanbul, [1995]), vol. 7, 527.

54   Muhammad Amin ibn Abidin, *Radd al-Muhtar ala ad-Dur al-Mukhtar*, (Dar al Marefa, [2004]), vol.4, 119; al-Jurjani, *Kitab at-Ta'rifat*, (Beirut: Matkabat Lebanon, 1978), 80.

55   Al-Hasan ibn Muhammad al-Nisaburi, *Ghara'ib al-Qur'an wa-Ragha-ib al-Furqan*, (Beirut: Dar al-Ma'rifa, 1992), vol. 9, 126.

56   Sadi Eren, *Cihad ve Savaş*, (İstanbul: Nesil, 1996) 30.

57   Ali Bulaç, 'Cihat,' *Yeni Ümit*, 63(2004): 45.

58   M. Fethullah Gülen, *İ'la-yi Kelimetullah veya Cihad*, (İzmir: Nil Yayınları, 1997), 5; M. Fethullah Gülen, *Asrın Getirdiği Tereddütler*, (İzmir: Nil Yayınları, 1998), vol.3, 219.

restricted to 'war') while the other is struggling against one's self or ego (*nafs*). Both of these dimensions can be grounded on different verses from the Qur'an and also on texts from the Sunnah. The Prophetic *hadith* (saying) meaning 'The real *mujahid* [one engaged in *jihad*] is one who struggles against his *nafs*,'[59] and the Prophet's (pbuh) remark when returning from a war, 'We have returned from the lesser *jihad* [armed struggle] to the greater *jihad*,'[60] express the *nafs* dimension of *jihad*. In the latter *hadith*, when his Companions asked what the greater *jihad* was, the Prophet (pbuh) replied:

> The believer's struggle against his own *nafs*.[61]

Therefore, the greater *jihad* means that one is always at war within oneself. One must struggle against all destructive emotions such as rancour, hatred, jealousy, arrogance, pride, self-love, egotism and the evil-commanding self (*al-nafs al-ammara*). This is a truly difficult and laborious endeavour.[62] That is why it is called the greater *jihad*.

The following verses show the war dimension of *jihad*, which is the lesser dimension or lesser part of it:

> Strive hard for God as is His due. (*al-Hajj*, 22:78)

> So go out, no matter whether you are lightly or heavily armed, and struggle in God's way with your possessions and your persons: this is better for you, if you only knew. (*al-Tawba*, 9:41)

> You who believe, shall I show you a bargain that will save you from painful torment? Have faith in God and His Messenger and struggle for His cause with your possessions and your persons – that is better for you, if you only knew. (*al-Saff*, 61:10–11).

The Prophet's (pbuh) answer to the question whether there is an act of worship that is equivalent to *jihad* also proves this dimension:

---

59   Al Tirmidhi, *Jami al-Tirmidhi*, Fada'il al Jihad, hadith no. 2; Abu `Abd Allah Ahmad ibn Muhammad ibn Hanbal al-Shaybani, *Musnad*, vol.6, 20-22.

60   Isma'il b. Muhammad al-'Ijlouni, *Kashf al-Khafa'*, Cairo, vol.1, 424.

61   Ali ibn Sultan al-Qari, *Asrar al-Marfu'ah fi Akhbar al-Mawdu'ah*, 127; see also Ali al-Muttagi, *Kanz al-Ummal*, vol. 4, 616; Ibrahim al-Bajuri, *Hashiya al-Bajuri ala Sharh ibn Qasim*, vol.2, 265.

62   Gülen, *Asrın Getirdiği Tereddütler*, vol.3, 206.

I have not found an act of worship that is equivalent to *jihad*. When a *mujahid* goes on an expedition, would you be able to go to a mosque, pray constantly and fast without breaking off until he returns?[63]

He also said that there was no equivalent to the '*jihad* of one who fights against the idolaters with his property and person.'[64]

It is possible to add other dimensions to *jihad* in addition to struggle against the enemy and the *nafs* based on the following *hadiths*:

A person who works for the good of widows and the helpless is like those who fight in the name of God.[65]

The most virtuous *jihad* is speaking truth to a despotic and tyrannical ruler's face.[66]

Jihad also has a social and intellectual dimension in the context of exerting conscience and reason to derive a legal ruling from the sources, a process called *ijtihad*, from the same root as *jihad*. So we see that while the Qur'an certainly does authorise the war dimension of *jihad* in its proper context, this is only one element of a multi-faceted Islamic concept.

More importantly, even when *jihad* means war, Islamic legal scholars attached stringent conditions to it based on the teachings of the Qur'an and Sunnah. These conditions were set out in a previous section ('How should we understand verses in the Qur'an which command war against unbelievers?: *Conclusions*').

If the two concepts are correctly understood, there is no contradiction between *jihad* and dialogue. The greater *jihad*, the struggle against the *nafs*, of course *facilitates* dialogue by making the individual more humble, gentle, compassionate and empathetic. The forms of *jihad* mentioned above, that is, working for the poor and the helpless, and speaking out against injustice, may be served by dialogue, because dialogue can help different religious and cultural communities to combine forces in such good works.

---

63 Al-Bukhari, *Sahih al-Bukhari*, Jihad, hadith nos. 1, 2; Muslim ibn al-Hajjaj, *Sahih Muslim*, Imara, hadith no. 110; Kamil Miras, *Tecrid-i Sarih Muhtasarı, Sahih-i Buhari Tercümesi*, (Ankara: Başbakanlık Basımevi, 1966), vol.8, 256. For a similar hadith see, Abu Bakr al-'Abasi ibn Abi Shayba, *Al-Musannaf*, ch. 5, hadith no. 287.

64 Abu Dawud, *Sunan Abu Dawud*, Witr, hadith no. 12.

65 Al-Bukhari, *Sahih al-Bukhari*, Nafaqat, hadith no. 1; Muslim, *Sahih Muslim*, Zuhd, hadith no. 41.

66 Abu Dawud, *Sunan Abu Dawud*, Melahim, hadith no. 17.

The concept of the lesser *jihad*, *jihad* as armed conflict, does not imply that dialogue is not a valid concept within Islam. The two simply apply in different situations. In a situation of peaceful intercultural relations, for which the Prophet (pbuh) himself strove from the time of the Medina Charter and indeed before, dialogue is an entirely Islamically correct form of interaction with people of other cultures and faiths. Dialogue should serve the maintenance of that entirely desirable state of peaceful co-existence, promoting harmonious relations and addressing any tensions that arise. *Jihad* in the sense of armed struggle has its place in Muslim conduct when it is required for self-defence or to prevent oppression, and when war is declared by the state. One is justified, essentially, in taking up arms to protect one's faith, person, family, property and land from attack, when war has been properly declared. However, if tensions and conflicts can be resolved without force through dialogue and diplomacy, *jihad* in the sense of armed conflict does not apply.

In Islamic law, apostasy from Islam (*irtidad*) is punishable by death. How can this be reconciled with freedom of religion and the spirit of dialogue?

Irtidad, according to its dictionary definition, means to retreat, to return, or to leave. In Islamic terminology, it means to quit one's faith (*iman*), and to quit Islam, that is, to apostatise. A *murtad* is a person who undertakes *irtidad*, that is, someone who converts out of Islam, an apostate.

Is *irtidad*, changing one's religious beliefs, a crime? From an Islamic point of view, to consider apostasy a capital crime is against the fundamentals of the religion; it goes against the letter and spirit of several verses of the Qur'an, like 'There is no compulsion in religion,' and 'let those who wish to believe in it [the truth] do so, and let those who wish to reject it do so,' (*al-Baqara*, 2:256 and *al-Kahf*, 18:29). Furthermore, no worldly punishment for apostasy is mentioned anywhere in the Qur'an. The traditional position that *irtidad* is punishable by death in Islam is an *ijtihad*, that is, a scholarly opinion or interpretation, based largely on a few isolated *hadiths*:

The first is, 'Whoever changed his religion, kill him' (al-Bukhari, *Sahih al-Bukhari*, vol. 9, bk 84, hadith no. 56), the primary source for the traditional position on apostasy in Islam. The second is, 'The blood of a Muslim who confesses that there is no god but Allah and that I am the messenger of Allah, cannot be shed except in three cases: a life for a life; a married person who commits illegal sexual intercourse; and the one who turns renegade from Islam (apostate) and leaves the community of Muslims.'[67] The third is an incident in which some people from the 'Uraynah tribe came to the Prophet (pbuh) and became Muslim. As they found the Medinan climate uncongenial and became unwell, the Prophet (pbuh) advised them to spend some time in a place where the camels belonging to the public purse were kept, outside Medina. As soon as they were better, they murdered the shepherds appointed to them by the Prophet (pbuh) and stole the camels belonging to the public purse. When the Prophet (pbuh) heard this, he had them captured and killed in accordance with *al-Ma'ida*, 5:33, which was revealed upon this occasion.[68]

The first *hadith* is *ahad*:[69] it is narrated by only one person, namely Ibn Abbas. For the *hadith* to necessitate the death penalty for apostasy when the Qur'an provides no form of temporal punishment whatsoever, the *hadith* should at least be *mashhur*.[70] [71] What is more, when the matter is considered holistically, that is taking the Qur'an and body of Sunnah into account, it is clear that what the Prophet is referring to are incidents of apostasy undertaken by people who specifically intend to fight against and divide the Muslim community. This category of apostasy will be discussed further below.

There are a number of versions of the second *hadith*. The one narrated by A'ishah sheds light on the probable intention of the Prophet (pbuh) in his original saying. While the version given above prescribes temporal punishment for 'the one who turns renegade from Islam (apostate) and leaves the community of Muslims,' A'ishah is more specific. Her version states: 'And a man who leaves Islam *and engages in fighting against Allah and*

---

67 Al-Bukhari, *Sahih al-Bukhari*, Diyat, hadith no. 6. Muslim, *Sahih Muslim*, Kitab al-Qasama, hadith no. 4152.

68 Al-Bukhari, *Sahih al-Bukhari*, Muharibun, hadith no. 2; *Al-Maida* 5:33-34 reads as follows: 'Those who wage war against God and His Messenger and spread corruption in the land should be punished by death, crucifixion, the amputation of an alternate hand and foot, or banishment from the land: a disgrace for them in this world, and then a terrible punishment in the Hereafter, unless they repent before you overpower them – in that case bear in mind that God is forgiving and merciful.'

69 A *hadith* which is *ahad* (literally, 'single') is one reported by only one, two, or three different narrators of the same generation.

70 A *hadith* which is *mashhur* (literally, 'well-known') is one reported by several narrators and transmitted through several chains of narration, though through fewer chains than a hadith which is *mutawatir*. The term *mutawatir* (literally, 'reported by many from many') refers to a *hadith* which was reported by many narrators in the same generation and passed down through many chains of narration.

71 This *hadith* is discussed further in Ahmet Kurucan, *İslam'da Düşünce Özgürlüğü*, (Zaman Kitap, 2007), 145-6.

His Prophet shall be executed, crucified or exiled [our italics].'[72] Reading the first version in light of the second it is apparent that it is the treacherous 'fighting against' Allah, his Prophet (pbuh) and the Muslim community that is punished, not the mere renunciation of faith.[73]

As for the incident concerning some people from the 'Uraynah tribe, they received capital punishment for murdering the innocent shepherds (and stealing from the public purse). This incident is one of murder, robbery and mutiny rather than a mere renunciation of faith.

To understand the Prophet's (pbuh) approval of the death penalty in particular cases of apostasy (there were very few cases of apostasy in any event), and to understand the adoption of this penalty as standard by jurists and scholars, we must refer to the intimate connection of religious and political identity in the early Islamic *ummah*. Punishments came to be associated with *irtidad* in contexts in which it was essentially being treated as a political issue. When we consider early Islamic history we see that individuals and groups who left the fold of Islam were not only leaving their beliefs, but, almost always, were also joining groups that were actively waging war against the Muslims. As a result, the form of *irtidad* which was punished in the time of the Prophet (pbuh) was one that involved high treason, not the form of *irtidad* which was a mere renunciation of faith. There is no record of any person being punished with the death penalty for simply renouncing his Islamic faith during the time of the Prophet (pbuh). As far as we are aware, there is only one incident during the time of the Prophet (pbuh) which can be deemed as mere renunciation of faith. The following is an account of that incident in *Sahih al-Bukhari*:

> A Bedouin gave the Pledge of Allegiance to Allah's Apostle for Islam. Then the Bedouin got fever at Medina, came to Allah's Apostle and said, 'O Allah's Apostle! Cancel my Pledge!' But Allah's Apostle refused. Then he came to him (again) and said, 'O Allah's Apostle! Cancel my Pledge!' But the Prophet refused. Then he came to him (again) and said, 'O Allah's Apostle! Cancel my Pledge.' But the Prophet refused. The Bedouin finally went out (of Medina), whereupon Allah's Apostle said, 'Medina is like

---

72   Abu Duwad, *Sunan Abu Dawud*, bk 33, hadith 4339.

73   See also Abdullah Saeed and Hassan Saeed, *Freedom of Religion, Apostasy and Islam*, (Ashgate, 2004), 58 ff.

a pair of bellows (furnace): it expels its impurities and brightens and clears its good.' (Al-Bukhari, *Sahih al-Bukhari*, vol. 9, hadith no. 318)

As is shown, the Prophet (pbuh) considered the Bedouin's renunciation of Islam as a matter of free will and personal choice; the Bedouin was permitted to leave Medina without any repercussions whatsoever. Thus we see that, in accordance with the Qur'an's stance on freedom of religion, the Prophet (pbuh) did not approve temporal punishment for renunciation of Islam per se, but rather for those acts of renunciation which involved treason.

After the Prophet's (pbuh) time, apostasy continued to be almost inseparable from treason. During the reign of Abu Bakr, communities abandoned Islam and rose against the central government; while renouncing their faith they were also engaging in political acts of rebellion against the state. Punishments inflicted on such people at that time, and in other eras when comparable political conditions prevailed, were effectively punishments for high treason, not for the renouncement of religious beliefs. This argument is strengthened by the Hanafi school's teaching that a woman apostate is not punishable by death because she cannot take up arms against Muslims. In addition, in books on jurisprudence we find that the matter of *irtidad* and associated punishments has been considered by scholars as a political issue and classed under international relations and the measures to be taken during times of war.

Irtidad came to be considered a capital crime because it was identified with the grave act of treason which generally accompanied it in the context of early Islamic history. This categorisation of *irtidad* as a capital crime was not given in the Qur'an; the categorisation of *irtidad* in the form of mere renunciation of faith as a capital crime was not part of the Sunnah either. The position of categorising *irtidad* as a capital crime is an *ijtihad* of the classical scholars and jurists. Since apostasy no longer implies high treason and political rebellion as it did when the traditional *ijtihad* was formulated, and since that *ijtihad* is at odds with clear teachings from the Qur'an and the Sunnah, it can be superseded by a new *ijtijad* today.

Chapter 3

The Basis from the Prophet's Life

Approaching the Sunnah

The Prophet (pbuh) is the communicator and interpreter of the Qur'an. His Sunnah is the essential resource without which the Qur'an could not be understood correctly. The Sunnah is the second main source of Islam after the Qur'an. Like the Qur'an it is binding upon all the Muslims, and they need to refer to it, alongside the Qur'an, until the end of time.

The Prophet's (pbuh) life was spent in dialogue with atheists, idolaters and People of the Book. Treaties, friendly relations and commercial partnerships are all facets of this dialogue. His examples, in this area as in every other, are precious treasures for Muslims, who accept him as a model and a guide.

To follow the example of the Prophet (pbuh) faithfully we need to adopt an attitude of intellectual inquiry when learning from the Sunnah. Deriving lessons from his behaviour to apply to our times and to guide our actions is only possible through such a critical approach.

If we fail to examine the social, political, economic, cultural and religious background of events, we will not achieve a proper understanding of the Sunnah. To arrive at a correct and relevant understanding we must consider not only *how* the Prophet (pbuh) acted but also *why* he did as he did. In asking *why* we move from unthinking imitation of the Prophet's (pbuh) external actions to reflection on the internal intentions which give those actions their meaning and value. Since the Prophet (pbuh) is an example for us for all times, his example cannot be imprisoned within the time frame in which he lived. But the Prophet's (pbuh) intentions and motivations would not be expressed by the same actions and words in dissimilar circumstances. It is inquiry into the *why* of the Sunnah that enables us to understand the intention behind the Prophet's (pbuh) actions, allowing us to imitate his intentions today while adapting the actions through which they were expressed to our times and circumstances. If we do not go through this process of reflection, following the Sunnah of the Prophet (pbuh) would require us to replicate the conditions prevalent in his lifetime, fifteen centuries ago, which is not possible.

In this chapter, we consider the Prophet's (pbuh) relationships with people of other faiths in his life in Mecca and Medina from this perspective so that he, as a model, can illuminate our present with his behaviour.

What are the main features of the Prophet's (pbuh) relationship with the People of the Book?

The Prophet (pbuh) recognised justice and honour in non-Muslim groups and individuals and entered into friendly relationships with those who displayed these qualities. The Muslims suffered severe persecution and torment at the hands of Meccan idolaters in the early period of Islam. The Prophet (pbuh) suggested to those who wanted to escape this persecution, which could amount to murder when Muslims refused to convert back to their ancestors' religion, that they should temporarily migrate to Abyssinia. The Prophet (pbuh) explained his preference for Abyssinia as follows:

> 'There is a king who loves justice and in whose territories nobody is oppressed.'[74]

The king (Najashi) that the Prophet (pbuh) described as one who did not persecute, Ashama ibn Abjar, was a Christian.

The Prophet (pbuh) entered into trade relationships with People of the Book. At the time of his death, a person of Medina belonging to the Jewish faith was in possession of a shield belonging to the Prophet (pbuh), which he had given as surety for a debt.[75] This shows that the Jewish people in Medina traded freely with their Muslim neighbours, and that the Prophet himself (pbuh) traded with his Jewish neighbours.

Further, he actively protected the rights and freedom of People of the Book, honoured those beliefs and traditions that he shared with them, and treated them with courtesy and respect. He visited the religious schools of the Jews

---

74   Muhammad Hamidullah, *The Life and Work of the Founder of Islam*, (Luton: Apex Books Concern, 1975), 46. A Turkish translation is also available. See: *İslam Peygamberi*, trans. Salih Tuğ, (İstanbul: İrfan Yayınları, 2004).), vol. 1, 117.

75   Al-Bukhari, *Sahih al-Bukhari*, Jihad, hadith no. 89.

(*Beit Midrash*) from time to time to ensure that there were no restrictions on their freedom to learn and teach their religion.[76] When a delegation of Christians from Najran came to negotiate a pact with the Prophet (pbuh), he courteously allowed them to pray in the mosque which lasted the whole day.[77]

It is a well known fact that the Muslims prayed towards Jerusalem for 17 months before God appointed the Ka'ba as the direction of Muslim prayer. This shows the importance of Bayt al-Maqdis in Islam, demonstrating the significance of beliefs and traditions shared with the People of the Book.[78] In addition, the Prophet (pbuh) preferred to resemble People of the Book rather than the idolaters in mundane matters that were not explicitly stipulated by the divine will. For example, he let his hair down over his forehead like People of the Book in opposition to the idolaters' practice of parting their hair over the forehead.[79]

In his personal relations with People of the Book he set an example of scrupulous good neighbourliness, compassion and generosity, regardless of religious identity. This is evidenced by al-Bukhari's account of the concern of 'Abdullah ibn 'Amr to share meat with his Jewish neighbour: 'Mujahid reported that a sheep was slaughtered for 'Abdullah ibn 'Amr. He asked his slave, 'Have you given any to our Jewish neighbour? Have you given any to our Jewish neighbour? I heard the Messenger of Allah, may Allah bless him and grant him peace, say, "Jibril kept on recommending that I treat my neighbours well until I thought that he would order me to treat them as my heirs."'[80] The Prophet (pbuh) was also ready to accept the hospitality of People of the Book, as in the case of a Jew in Medina (unnamed in the sources) whose dinner invitation he accepted.[81] He did not discriminate between people on the grounds of religious conviction when he visited the

---

76   'Abdallah b. 'Umar al-Baidawi, *Anwar al-Tanzeel*, (Cairo: 1330/1912), commentary on *al-Bakara*, 2:91.

77   Ibn Hisham, *As-Sirah an-Nabawiyyah*, vol. 2, 224; Hamidullah, *İslam Peygamberi*, vol. 2, 1086. Years later, when idolatry completely disappeared, he began to wear his hair with a middle parting again.

78   *Al-Bakara*, 2:144; Elmalılı, *Hak Dini Kur'an Dili*, vol. 1, 134ff.

79   Al-Bukhari, *Sahih al-Bukhari*, Manaqib, hadith no. 23, Libas, hadith no. 70; Muslim, *Sahih Muslim*, Fada'il, hadith no. 90; Abu Dawud, *Sunan Abu Dawud*, Tarajjul, hadith no. 10; Abu 'Abdillah Muhammad ibn Yazid ibn Majah, *Sunan ibn Majah*, Libas, hadith no. 36.

80   Al-Bukhari, *al-Adab al-Mufrad*, 'Neighbours', hadith no. 105. The translation used is by Ustadha Aisha Bewley; see 'Neighbours; Al-Adab al-Mufrad Al-Bukhari', SunniPath website, accessed 30th November 2011, http://www.sunnipath.com/library/Hadith/H0003P0006.aspx.

81   Ibn Hanbal, *Musnad*, vol.3, 210.

sick and when he gave spiritual and material support to people.[82]

In addition, when the funeral procession of a Jew passed by him on one occasion he showed his respect by standing up. When some of his companions questioned his action, pointing out that the deceased was a Jew, he replied by observing that the person was a human being, demonstrating his respect for his Jewish neighbours and indeed for all human persons as such.[83]

Finally, one of his last statements on his deathbed was:

> I entrust to you the Jews and Christians who are People of the Book.[84]

What this meant was that he wanted the Muslims to treat the People of the Book who lived under Muslim rule as *dhimmi*s (i.e. under a treaty of protection or *dhimma*) justly, as he had done in his lifetime, and not to persecute or insult them in a way unbecoming a Muslim.

These few examples show that our Prophet (pbuh) accepted non-Muslims from the beginning, and sought to enter into relations with them in the context of an environment of freedom of religion, a pluralist society, and a search for common ground.

He never discriminated among people on the basis of their religious identities. Any historical instance of such discrimination is the result of continuous animosity and attacks against Muslims by particular individuals. Otherwise, neither people belonging to the Christian or Jewish faith nor polytheists faced any discrimination. They were able to live in harmony under the Medina Charter.

---

82   Al-Bukhari, *Sahih al-Bukhari*, Janaiz, hadith no. 80.

83   Al-Bukhari, *Sahih al-Bukhari*, vol. 2, bk 23, hadith no. 398; vol 2, bk 23, hadith no. 399.

84   Abu Dawud, *Sunan Abu Dawud*, Imara, hadith no. 33.

Is the Medina Charter a project for co-existence, a basis for dialogue activities?

The Medina Charter is an agreement that the Prophet (pbuh) brokered between the Muslims and various Jewish and polytheistic tribes of Medina. Contrary to common belief, Muslims were not a majority when they migrated to Medina. In fact they were a minority of approximately 1,500 individuals. The majority community were the polytheists (around 4,500) and Jews (around 4,000). So the Muslims made up only about 15% of the population of Medina.

According to the Medina Charter, those different tribal, ethnic and religious groups who were signatories formed one 'ummah', that is a common political, economic, legal, military and social entity within which they could co-exist peacefully while retaining their respective identities. This Charter, which is similar, in structure, to a federation, guarantees peace, security, freedom, equality, justice and communal life founded on basic universal human values to all the signatory groups. It is possible to ground all the terms of the agreement in the Qur'an. It is noteworthy that political scientists today sometimes turn to the Medina Charter as a resource and model in their search for new political administrative models suited to the changing and developing world. The Medina Charter has also been the subject of many doctoral dissertations.

The Charter is a social contract that is not based on blood, language, religion, race or class distinctions and it shows that differences in faith do not constitute an obstacle to living together. The Charter, by which the Prophet (pbuh) is accepted as a leader and which serves as the constitution of the Medina city-state, is characterised by pluralism and freedom, quite different from the nation-state model which is built around a racial and linguistic community. It lays down the principle of mutual responsibility of the parties.[85] Its legal aspects include many regulations regarding legislative, executive and judiciary structures and its political aspects envision a pluralist and participant society. It was an important step towards making Medina, which had a chaotic tribal system before the Hijra (the emigration from Mecca to Medina), a more liveable place.

---

85 Muhammad 'Amara (/Umara), *İslam ve İnsan Hakları*, trans. Asım Kanar, (İstanbul: Denge Yayınları, 1992), 131. An English translation is available: 'Amara, Muhammad, *Islam and Human Rights: Requisite Necessities Rather than Mere Rights*, (Publications of the Islamic Educational, Scientific and Cultural Organization, 1996).

The Charter document regulates relations between different groups in a mixed society of Muslims, idolaters and Jews. At the beginning of the document the word 'ummah' occurs and seems to refer to the Muslims (local in Yathrib/Medina, and the emigrants from Mecca and elsewhere) as 'one community (ummah) to the exclusion of all men'. In Islamic terminology ummah refers to the world-wide community of Muslim believers. It was used by the Prophet (pbuh) and by the Qur'an to designate the community of believers. It has strong connotations of mutual support and service and of brotherhood.

The relationship intended between the groupings signatory to the Charter document, who had for many years lived in a state of perpetual inter-group conflict, may not have been quite the fellowship characterising a community bound together by a single belief system and ethos. Nevertheless, later in the document, precisely the term 'ummah' is applied in a much more inclusive way to the residents of Medina. One of the Jewish tribes in Yathrib is said to be 'one community ('ummah) with the believers' in political though not in religious terms. The statement is then extended to other Jewish tribes along with certain Arab clans and tribes: 'The Jews of the B[anu] 'Auf are one community (ummah) with the believers (the Jews have their religion and the Muslims have theirs) their freedmen and their persons except those who behave unjustly and sinfully, for they hurt but themselves and their families. The same applies to the Jews of the B. al-Najjar, B. al-Harith, B. Sai ida, B. Jusham, B. al-Aus, B. Tha'laba, and the Jafna, a clan of the Tha'laba and the B. al-Shutayba.'[86] The fact that the Charter applies the word 'ummah' to this composite, plural society does suggest that the Prophet (pbuh) at least envisaged parallels between the community of believers (men and women from different clans and tribes) and the diverse groupings in Medina. Those groupings were at least expected and intended to cultivate peace, co-operation and mutual trust in their relations.

Thus the Medina Charter provides an invaluable model of a system safeguarding the rights and freedoms of all and thereby providing a safe environment in which peace, co-operation and trust, and perhaps ultimately friendship and fellowship, can develop. We can define the Charter as:

---

86   See Appendix 1.

> A social structure that managed difference based on an
> agreement under principles that can be described as 'natural
> law'; which adhered to justice and equity in determining rights
> and duties; and which promoted common interests under a
> pluralist, participatory and unitary political umbrella based on
> lawfulness and equality before the law.[87]

Some commentators argue that the Muslims needed such an agreement
because they were weak when they first emigrated to Medina; they did not
need it after the Islamic city-state was established. Such commentators see
the Charter as a temporary means to the end of Muslim security, not as
securing a state of affairs desirable in itself, or as an enduring model for a
pluralist society. Such interpretations are not on firm ground when we look
at the issue in its entirety, considering the relevant material from the Qur'an
and Sunnah and relevant historical facts. The Qur'anic verses presented
above in 'The case for dialogue in the Qur'an' suggest that the religious
freedom, equality and inter-group dialogue promoted by the Medina
Charter are considered as inherently valuable in Islam, not just desirable as
a means to Muslim security. The fact that the Prophet (pbuh) abided by all
his agreements including the Medina Charter unless they were violated by
the other party, even during the most powerful periods of the Islamic state,
shows that his commitment to just and respectful inter-group relations was
fundamental, not a product of necessity. This conclusion is supported by the
fact that the Prophet (pbuh) made many similar agreements.

We should be cautious about arguing that the Medina Charter was Islam's
ultimate project of co-existence, providing for an ideal social order in every
respect from an Islamic perspective. However, it is certainly a project for co-
existence which has much enduring wisdom relevant to Muslims living in
diverse societies today.

The Charter demonstrates the Islamic desirability of just and harmonious
interfaith and intercultural relations. It points to the possibility of relationships
of peace, co-operation and trust, of friendship and fellowship, between
people of different faiths and cultures belonging to one 'ummah'. It gives an
inspiring and practical example of the kind of legal and political provisions
which make these relationships possible by enshrining religious freedom,

---

87   Atalay, *Doğu ve Batı Kaynaklarında Birlikte Yaşama*, 373.

equality and the rule of law as fundamental principles. In short, it affirms the personal and social goals of dialogue activities and provides guidance on the conditions in which these goals may be achieved. The Charter, which was first proposed and subsequently implemented and supervised by the Prophet (pbuh), is one of the most important sources of Islamic support for interfaith and intercultural dialogue.

What place do the Jews have in the Medina Charter?

The question about the status of the Jews in the Medina Charter, a document we have been discussing in the context of dialogue, arises because of the presumption that the Charter's provision could be interpreted differently with respect to Jews. The articles of the agreement pertaining to Jews are as follows:

> To the Jew who follows us belong help and equality. He shall not be wronged nor shall his enemies be aided. The peace of the believers is indivisible. [...]

> The Jews shall contribute to the cost of war so long as they are fighting alongside the believers. The Jews of the B[anu] 'Auf are one community with the believers (the Jews have their religion and the Muslims have theirs), their freedmen and their persons except those who behave unjustly and sinfully, for they hurt but themselves and their families.

> The same applies to the Jews of the B. al-Najjar, B. al-Harith, B. Sa'ida, B. Jusham, B. al-Aus, B. Tha'laba, and the Jafna, a clan of the Tha'laba and the B. al-Shutayba. Loyalty is a protection against treachery. The freedmen of Tha'laba are as themselves. The close friends of the Jews are as themselves.[88]

> None of them shall go out to war save with the permission of Muhammad, but he shall not be prevented from taking revenge for a wound. He who slays a man without warning slays himself

---

88 The constitution recognises the Arab custom of granting *aman* (security) to others. Therefore if a person is given security by a signatory of this constitution then that person will be treated by the other signatories (Muslims) as protected and afforded the rights provided therein. Even if that person who seeks security is an enemy of the Muslims he will be deemed to be under the *aman* of the Jewish person and protected accordingly.

and his household, unless it be one who has wronged him, for God will accept that.

The Jews must bear their expenses and the Muslims their expenses. Each must help the other against anyone who attacks the people of this document. [...]

If any dispute or controversy likely to cause trouble should arise it must be referred to God and to Muhammad the apostle of God. [...]

If they are called to make peace and maintain it they must do so; and if they make a similar demand on the Muslims it must be carried out except in the case of a holy war.[89]

Every one shall have his portion from the side to which he belongs. The Jews of al-Aus, their freedmen and themselves have the same standing with the people of this document in pure loyalty from the people of this document. Loyalty is a protection against treachery. He who acquires aught acquires it for himself. God approves of this document.[90]

This deed will not protect the unjust and the sinner. The man who goes forth to fight and the man who stays at home in the city is safe unless he has been unjust and sinned. God is the protector of the good and God-fearing man and Muhammad is the apostle of God.[91]

A number of things are clear from the text above quoted: the Jews are accepted as part of the one *ummah* (community) and their equal status with the other signatories is underlined; there are no restraints on any party in

---

89 We reproduce here the phrase ('holy war') used in the Guillaume translation being cited, despite its inappropriateness. An alternative reading of this clause is given on the Constitution Society website, 'Full Text of the Madina Charter,' accessed 10th November 2011, http://www.constitution.org/cons/medina/macharter.htm:

'If they (the parties to the Pact other than the Muslims) are called upon to make and maintain peace (within the State) they must do so. If a similar demand (of making and maintaining peace) is made on the Muslims, it must be carried out, except when the Muslims are already engaged in a war in the Path of Allah (so that no secret ally of the enemy can aid the enemy by calling upon Muslims to end hostilities under this clause).'

90 Muhammad Hamidullah, *Mecmua Wasaiq al-Siyasiyye*, (Beirut: Dar al-Nafais, 1985), 39-44.

91 'The Medina Charter', Constitution Society, accessed 30th May 2011, http://www.constitution.org/cons/medina/con_medina.htm. The text is taken from A. Guillaume, *The Life of Muhammad — A Translation of Ishaq's Sirat Rasul Allah*, (Oxford University Press, Karachi, 1955), 231-233.

respect of the religion they follow, rather there is freedom of religion; that has implications for the tolerance of multiple legal systems since religion was the basis for the principles and rules of personal law in that period; the Jews and others have to make some measure of common cause with their co-signatories, at very least not side against them in a military conflict; finally, in the event of a dispute between the signatory parties, there is an agreed higher authority to refer to, in this case the Prophet (pbuh).

Did the Prophet (pbuh) make agreements with non-Muslims other than the Medina Charter?

The Prophet (pbuh) made many other agreements with Jews, Christians and polytheists in addition to the Medina Charter. We will give just a few examples here.

The Prophet's (pbuh) agreement with the Najran Christians which allowed the Muslims to pray in their own *masjid* is a historical document of equal importance to the Medina Charter.[92] According to the agreement:

> No clergy's or monk's post shall be changed, nobody shall be denied travel, their places of worship shall not be destroyed or turned into Islamic *masjids* or added to Muslims' buildings. Whoever fails to follow these rules will be violating God's treaty and opposing His Messenger. No taxes [*jizya* – poll tax levied on *dhimmi*s (people living under a *dhimma*, protection treaty) or *kharaj* – land tax] shall be collected from priests, clergy, people who dedicate themselves to prayer, monks, or those who occupy themselves with worship in isolated places and mountains… No Christian shall be forced to convert to Islam; … 'Do not dispute with the People of the Book except by what is best.' They shall be treated with compassion wherever they are, no harm shall come to them… If a Christian woman joins (marries) a Muslim man of her own accord, the Muslim husband shall consent to her Christianity, allow her to fulfil her religious duties and shall not forbid her to do so. Whoever fails to do this and exerts pressure on her regarding her religion will be violating God's promise and His Messenger's treaty and he is

---

92 Ibn Hisham, *As-Sirah an-Nabawiyyah*, (Cairo: 1413/1992), vol. 2, 507; Muhammad ibn Sa'd, *Kitab Tabaqat al-Kubra*, (Beirut, [c.1960]), vol. 1, 357.

a liar before God… If they (Christians) need help from Muslims
with repairing their churches, monasteries or any other religious or
worldly business, Muslims shall help them without placing them
under any obligation; help and support for their religious needs
shall be provided out of abiding by the promise of God's Messenger,
as a donation and as God's grace.[93]

The agreement made with the Christian Ibn Harith bin Qa'b and his tribe
is another example. The following is a short excerpt from this agreement:

The religions, churches, life, honour and property of all
Christians living in the east and west are under the protection
of God, His Messenger and all believers. No Christian shall be
forced to convert to Islam. If any of the Christians are subject to
murder or any other injustice, Muslims must help them.[94]

There were agreements of the same kind with the people of Yemen and
Bahrain, granting religious freedom to Christians and guaranteeing that
their churches would not be touched and that their priests and bishops
would not be put under pressure to convert.[95]

However we evaluate these agreements, they present a key framework
within which the notion of 'People of the Book' can be understood and
give valuable examples of how relationships with them should be conducted.
They clearly show that according to Islamic values People of the Book are
not enemies. They are a people that have the right to live anywhere they
wish, maintaining their own religious, national and cultural identity, as long
as they do not violate universal human values, principles of co-existence or
commonly agreed political and legal rules.

93 Hamidullah, *Mecmua Wasaiq al-Siyasiyye*, 124-6.

94 Hamidullah, *Mecmua Wasaiq al-Siyasiyye*, 154-5.

95 Ahmad b. Yahya al-Baladhuri, *Futuh al Buldan*, trans. Mustafa Fayda, (Ankara, 1987), 99-113.

Did the Prophet (pbuh) enter into social and commercial relations with the People of the Book?

In addition to entering into peace agreements with the People of the Book, the Prophet (pbuh) also engaged in social and commercial relations with them. This section gives a few examples.

The Prophet (pbuh) had social, political, legal and economic relationships with the People of the Book, especially in Medina. He did so without compromising his religious duties.[96] For example, based on the Qur'an's permission, the Prophet (pbuh) shared the food of the People of the Book.[97]

After Khaybar, the Prophet (pbuh) married Safiya bint Huyayy, daughter of a leader of the Jewish tribe Banu Nadir. Although it is debated whether or not Safiya had converted to Islam before she married, this marriage is significant in any case: it proves that Safiya's Jewish heritage at the least, or her continuing Jewish faith at the most, did not constitute an obstacle to the Prophet's (pbuh) marrying her. In any event, Islam permits Muslim men to marry women from among the People of the Book.

As for commercial relations, reliable traditions report that the Prophet (pbuh) put his armour in pawn with a Jew in exchange for provisions,[98] that 'Ali had a joint business with a Jewish jeweller, selling a certain herb,[99] and that some Companions of the Prophet (pbuh) asked for his help to pay off their debts after doing business with Jews.[100]

Because popular books in circulation mainly focus on relations between Muslims and people of other religions in terms of an animosity–war–peace triangle, social, cultural and trade relations that are central to an understanding of interfaith relations in Islam have frequently been ignored

---

96   Osman Güner, *Resulullah'ın Ehli Kitapla Münasebetleri*, (Ankara: Fecr Yayıncılık, 1997), 344.

97   Al-Bukhari, Sahih al-Bukhari, Hibe, hadith no. 26, Maghazi, hadith no. 41, Tibb, hadith no. 55; Abu Dawud, *Sunan Abu Dawud*, At'ima, hadith no. 20, Diyat, hadith no. 6.

98   Al-Bukhari, *Sahih al-Bukhari*, Buyu, hadith no. 14, Rehn, hadith no. 2, Istikraz, hadith no. 2; Muslim, *Sahih Muslim*, Musaqat, hadith no. 124; al Tirmidhi, *Jami al-Tirmidhi*, Buyu, hadith no. 7.

99   Al-Bukhari, *Sahih al-Bukhari*, Buyu, hadith no. 28, Musaqat, hadith no. 14; Abu Dawud, *Sunan Abu Dawud*, Harac, hadith no. 20.

100 Al-Bukhari, *Sahih al-Bukhari*, Buyu, hadith no. 51; Muslim, *Sahih Muslim*, Musaqat, hadith no. 91; Abu Dawud, *Sunan Abu Dawud*, Wasaya, hadith no. 17, Buyu, hadith no. 13.

or dismissed.[101] One reason for this might well be the existence of something of a strained relationship between Muslim-majority countries and the West over the last centuries. Nevertheless, in the context of democratisation processes in the Muslim world and the renewed prominence of human rights issues, scholarly attention has turned to the importance of cultural, social and trade relations between Muslims and people of other faiths, both historically and in the contemporary world. A good number of doctoral dissertations have recently been written on this topic.

How should we understand the exile of Jews from Medina, and the wars against the Jewish tribes such as Khaybar and Banu Qurayza?

The principles that applied in political relations with the idolaters also apply here. The Prophet (pbuh) defended the Muslim community and engaged in military response when the idolaters violated treaty terms, tried to convert Muslims by force, oppression, torture or usurpation and tried to deprive people of their most essential right to life through conspiracies and military attacks. The Jews who co-operated with the idolaters in this process or who independently behaved in the same way were met with a similar response.

A number of Jewish leaders and tribes violated the Medina Charter by engaging in these kinds of treacherous activity. As Ibn Ishaq reports, the Jews of Banu Qaynuqa violated the Charter by attacking a Muslim woman in the bazaar.[102] A passing Muslim defended the woman, the man who had attacked her was killed and hostilities between the two groups escalated. Banu Qaynuqa refused to respect the Charter and appeal to the arbitration of the Prophet (pbuh), instead planning hostilities against the Muslims and calling for reinforcements from their allies.[103] In the face of this aggression, the Prophet (pbuh) had little choice but to expel the tribe from Medina.[104]

Banu Nadir plotted an assassination attempt on the Prophet (pbuh), violating

---

101 A few of the many examples of recent books focused on the animosity-war-peace triangle are as follows: Samuel P Huntington, *The Clash of Civilizations and the Remaking of the World Order*, (Simon and Schuster, 1996); Bernard Lewis, *Islam and the West*, (OUP, 1994); Roger Crowley, *1453: the Holy War for Constantinople and the Clash of Islam and the West*, (Hyperion, 2006); Benazir Bhutto, *Reconciliation: Islam, Democracy and the West*, (Harper, 2008); Gilles Kapel and Pascale Ghazaleh, *The War for Muslim Minds: Islam and the West*, (Belknap Press of Harvard University Press, 2006).

102 Muhammad Hamidullah, *Hz. Peygamber'in Savaşları*, trans. Salih Tuğ, (İstanbul: Yağmur Yayınları, 2002), 203.

103 Martin Lings, *Muhammad: His Life Based on the Earliest Sources*, (New York: Inner Traditions, 1987), 161.

104 Ibn Qayyim al-Jawziyyah, *Zad al Maad*, (Cairo: Muhammad Hamid al-Faqqi, 1373/1953), vol. 2, 230.

the Medina Charter and threatening not only the life of the Prophet (pbuh) but the security and wellbeing of the whole society.[105] It was for this reason that they were expelled from Medina. They later put longstanding plots against the Muslims into practice at the Battle of the Trench.[106]

The war with Khaybar related to the treacherous behaviour of the Banu Nadir, who took refuge with the Jews of Khaybar after their expulsion from Medina. From this new base they continued to plot against the Muslims, eliciting support from the Jews from Khaybar, the Quraish in Mecca and a range of local Arab tribes who were either persuaded or bribed to join the conspiracy.[107] The war against Khaybar was thus clearly waged to defend the Muslims and their allies in Medina.

The killing of the men of the Banu Qurayza, reported by Ibn Ishaq, was, once again, the end result of a violation of the Medina Charter. During the Battle of the Trench the Banu Qurayza chose to consort with the invading Meccan army against the Muslims, abandoning their pact and effectively engaging in high treason. They later surrendered to the Muslim community that they had betrayed. Their fate was decided by an arbitrator chosen from amongst their allies in the Banu Aws, according to the regulations of their own scripture, the Torah.[108]

In each case the tribes in question failed to abide by the political treaties they signed. They approached Muslims with active hostility and secretly conspired, through plots, assassination attempts and intrigues, to destroy the Muslims. As a result, the Prophet (pbuh) responded according to the terms of the treaties that they had violated and in defence of the security and freedom of the Muslims and their allies.

The Prophet (pbuh) did not treat those Jews who did not violate the treaty with hostility, proving that his decisions to expel or fight particular groups were political decisions relating to groups of people who had expressly violated the terms of a peace treaty. Those who had not continued to enjoy the same status and security in Medina as they had done previously.

---

105 Hamidullah, *Hz. Peygamber'in Savaşları*, 206; Ibn Hisham, *As-Sirah an-Nabawiyyah*, (Dar al-Turas al-Arabiyya, 1971), vol. 2, 190.

106 Hamidullah, *Hz. Peygamber'in Savaşları*, 290.

107 Lings, *Muhammad: His Life Based on the Earliest Sources*, 215ff., Muhammad Hamidullah, *The Battlefields of the Prophet Muhammad*, (Luton: Apex Books, 1975), 34, 48.

108 Lings, *Muhammad: His Life Based on the Earliest Sources*, 220ff, 231. The relevant passage of Jewish Scripture is Deuteronomy 20:10-14.

Is the Prophetic *hadith* 'I was ordered to fight with people until they say 'There is no god but God,' [109] evidence that unbelief can be a *casus belli*?

According to the consensus of *hadith* scholars, the 'people' in the *hadith* refers to Arab idolaters.[110] In Imam al-Nasa'i's account, the same *hadith* has '*mushriqin*' (polytheists or unbelievers) instead of the word '*nas*' (people), which gives credit to this interpretation.[111] The Arab idolaters were hostile to the Prophet (pbuh) and the Muslims from the advent of the religion to the Prophet's (pbuh) death. In other words, they were constantly at war with the Muslims. Therefore this *hadith* is a statement against the enemy in a state of war.

To interpret this *hadith* as making unbelief a *casus belli* would introduce a contradiction to the main sources of Islam: the *hadith* as thus interpreted would contradict the Islamic principle of freedom of religion that is repeatedly affirmed in the Qur'an. The next chapter, which concerns itself with Islamic history, clearly shows that Muslim rulers in the course of fifteen centuries have adhered to the principle of freedom of religion.

What did the Prophet (pbuh) teach about the significance of ethnic difference?

In the following *hadith* the Prophet (pbuh) teaches that the fact that people belong to different ethnic or social groups should not be used as a means of establishing superiority of one over another. Superiority is to be measured not according to God-given characteristics such as race or lineage, but only according to the worth that people gain through their own effort of heedfulness and wariness of God, which the Qur'an terms '*taqwa*':

> O people! Remember that your Lord is one, your father [i.e. Adam] is one. An Arab is not superior over a non-Arab nor a non-Arab is superior over an Arab; also a white is not superior over a black nor a black is superior over a white except by *taqwa* [piety, Godfearing]. (Ibn Hanbal, *Musnad*, vol. 5, 411).

---

109 Al-Bukhari, *Sahih al-Bukhari*, Iman, hadith no. 18, Salat, hadith no. 28; Abu Dawud, *Sunan Abu Dawud*, Jihad, hadith no. 104; Muslim ibn al-Hallaj, *Sahih Muslim*, Iman, hadith no. 33.

110 Abu Abdullah Muhammad ibn Idris al-Shafi'i, *Kitab al-Umm*, (Beirut: Dar al-Fikr, 1983), vol. 4, 186; al-Jassas al-Razi, *Ahkam al-Qur'an*, vol. 1, 453.

111 Ahmad ibn Shu`ayb ibn Alī ibn Sīnān Abū `Abd ar-Rahmān al-Nasa'i, *Sunan an-Nasa'i*, Tahrim, hadith no. 1.

Chapter 4

The Historical Basis

The significance of examples from Islamic history

The historical practices and Islamic traditions of the Four Righteous Caliphs after the Prophet's (pbuh) time, and of the Umayyads, Abbasids, Seljuks and Ottomans, are important sources of evidence for our argument. These practices, along with political, economic and cultural arrangements showing the interpretation of Islamic norms by Islamic scholars in different historical circumstances, constitute a rich roadmap for us today. An Islamic approach certainly does not allow us to disclaim this heritage. It is a duty rather than an optional good to look at historical phenomena, without turning them into matters of doctrine, to explain what requires an explanation and to point out where the teachings of Islam have been misunderstood and thus incorrectly applied.

We contend, in this book, that the Qur'an and Sunnah make positive, peaceful, respectful intercultural engagement a religious duty for Muslims. This chapter highlights a small selection of the wealth of examples from Islamic history which show this religious duty being carried out faithfully during periods of Muslim rule. We try to highlight the relations of dialogue entered into by our ancestors by quoting some of the articles of the treaties of protection (*dhimma*) entered into during the rule of the Umayyads, Abbasids, Seljuks and Ottomans.

We recognise that Islamic history has not been an uninterrupted story of tolerance and respect. Muslim rulers and administrations have not always lived up to the teachings of the Qur'an and the Sunnah. Since history is a mine of lessons to take into the future, it is well worth examining such cases in detail, understanding the historical contexts in which they occurred and how the teachings of the Qur'an and Sunnah came to be overlooked or incorrectly applied. Unfortunately, that is beyond the scope of this book.

We can only note here that not every single military campaign waged by the increasingly powerful forces of early Islamic caliphates was in legitimate defence of Muslim persons, religious freedom, property or land against active aggression and after diplomacy had failed. We maintain that the Prophet (pbuh) only waged wars under these conditions, or according to the terms of treaties broken by other parties. The Four Righteous Caliphs also sought to keep warfare within the limits laid down in the Qur'an, with the additional guide of the practice of the Prophet (pbuh). However, later Islamic administrations, including some of the Abbasid and Ottoman administrations, did not in every instance adhere so carefully to the principles of these guides. Wars were, at times, waged in order to expand territory or for booty. Such wars are in no way justified by the Qur'an or Sunnah.

We do not argue that non-Muslims living under Muslim rule were at all times treated with justice and respect. It must, indeed, be recognised that difficulties were put in the way of non-Muslim subjects after the trauma of the Crusades and other wars, including wars between different Muslim groups.

This is by no means to imply that a fuller treatment of intercultural relations in Islamic history would be detrimental to our argument for dialogue. We do not offer our examples of positive intercultural engagement against a backdrop of pervasive failure, but in the context of an impressive level of general success. Even the most cynical critic of empire would have to concede that – whether it is a question of how the conquered fared, how diverse minorities fared, how slaves fared, how the economic and intellectual-cultural wealth of empire was shared – the rule of Islam was, compared to the rule of Romans or Persians before or the empires of the European nation-states afterwards, generally a force for good. Under Muslim rule non-Muslims retained their languages, cultures and religions to a degree not found under any other imperial rule than the Islamic. This cannot be explained except by recourse to the inherently Islamic values, central to our argument for dialogue, of recognising all people as legal persons with specific rights and duties, which the (Islamic) law of the land was supposed to respect and usually did. History in fact demonstrates that fundamental Islamic values, including the justice, tolerance, respect and good neighbourliness essential to dialogue, have an impressive capacity to survive the vicissitudes of history. Conquering and being conquered are transient historical situations, whereas the enduring reality of Islam is composed of precisely the values that the argument of this book seeks to highlight.

The scope of this book does not allow us to do more than sketch the wider context of the examples of positive intercultural engagement given in this chapter. For all its limitations, this sketch and the ensuing examples should provide at least a flavour of how the Islamic values of justice, tolerance, respect and good neighbourliness were successfully lived out in Islamic history, and what they meant to societies under Muslim rule.

Are there any events or treaties from Muslim history that lend support to dialogue?

There are many agreements and practices through which non-Muslims were accepted with their own religious and cultural values and enabled to live a comfortable life on Muslim lands during the reign of the Four Righteous Caliphs and of the Umayyads, Abbasids, Seljuks and Ottomans. Such practices, followed in states of war as in states of peace, earned the appreciation, admiration and astonishment of others.

In order to give some insight into these approaches, upon which entire books and theses have been written, we will mention just a few examples:

1. Upon his arrival at Jerusalem after the conquest to receive the keys to the city, Caliph 'Umar refused the invitation to pray in the Ba'th (Qiyamah) church or the Constantine church next to it. He was concerned that future generations might turn the churches into mosques to commemorate his prayer.[112]

    An excerpt from the agreement that Caliph 'Umar signed with the people of Aylah: 'This is an assurance of peace and protection given by the servant of Allah, Omar, Commander of the Believers, to the people of Ilia' (Jerusalem). He gave them an assurance of protection for their lives, property, church and crosses as well as the sick and healthy and all their religious community.

---

112 Abbas Mahmud al-Aqqad, *Majmu'at al-Abqariyat al-Islamiyah*, (Beirut: 1968), 427; Mustafa Fayda, *Hz. Ömer Zamanında Gayr-i Müslimler*, (İstanbul: Marmara Üniversitesi İlahiyat Fakültesi Yayınları, 1989), 171.

Their churches shall not be occupied, demolished nor taken
away wholly or in part. None of their crosses nor property
shall be seized. They shall not be coerced in their religion
nor shall any of them be injured.'[113]

2. When 'Umar saw a poor old *dhimmi* [person subject to a
    dhimma – treaty of protection] who was begging on the
    street to make a living, he said, 'We cannot leave you alone
    in your old age when we collected *jizya* [poll tax levied on
    dhimmis] from you in your youth.' He allocated a pension
    to needy *dhimmis* from the state's treasury.[114] He also ordered
    that his successors also protect the rights of the *dhimmis*.[115]
    This approach embodies Islam's respect and concern for all
    people on the basis of their humanity, regardless of religion.
    This attitude requires Islamic states to deal with all citizens
    according to principles of social justice.[116]

3. 'Umar ordered that the Christians of Damascus who were
    suffering from leprosy be given a share of the alms tax
    (*zakah*) paid by the Muslim population.[117]

4. When Abu 'Ubaidah ibn al-Jarrah was the governor of
    Damascus, news reached the city that the Byzantine Empire
    was preparing a major campaign against the Muslims. Upon
    hearing the news, some *dhimmis* living under Muslim rule
    in Damascus sent spies to communicate the information to
    Abu 'Ubaidah. Abu 'Ubaidah was worried that he would
    not be able to protect the lives and property of the *dhimmis*
    in the situation of the time and returned the *jizya* (poll tax
    collected from *dhimmis*, partly to provide them with security
    of life and property) he had collected from them, telling
    them that they were free to do as they pleased. Moved by this
    justice and tolerance, the Christians supported the Muslims
    in the war and prayed for their victory although they shared

113 Al-Tabari, *Annals of the Prophets and Kings*, (Brill, 2010), vol. 3, 105.

114 Ibn Qayyim al-Jawziyyah, *Ahkâm ahl al-Dhimma*, (Damascus: Matbaa Jami'a Dimashq, 1381/1961), vol. 1, 38.

115 Yaqub ibn Ibrahim Abu Yusuf, *Kitab al-Kharaj*, (Cairo: 1962), 144.

116 Yunus Vehbi Yavuz, *İslam'da Düşünce ve İnanç Özgürlüğü*, (İstanbul: Sahaflar Yayıncılık, 1994), 156.

117 Ahmad b. Yahya al-Baladhuri, *Kitab Futuh al-Buldan*, (Beirut: Dar al-Ma'arif, 1987), 177.

the faith of the Byzantine Christians. They renewed their *dhimma* agreement after the victory. A Nestorian priest describes his feelings in a letter to a friend as follows:

> These Tayites (Arabs), whom God has accorded domination in these days, have also become our masters; but they do not combat the Christian religion at all: on the other hand, they protect our faith, respect our priests and saints and make donations to our churches and our convents.[118]

5. When 'Amr ibn al-'As was the governor of Egypt, his son raced against a Copt and the Copt beat him. 'Amr's son could not bear his defeat and whipped the Coptic youth. The Copt complained about this to 'Umar, who sent for the governor and his son. When they arrived, he gave the Copt a whip and asked him to hit the governor's son as the governor's son had hit him. Then he said: 'Now whip 'Amr, because his son whipped you out of his trust in his father's office.' A'mr objected, saying that it was his son, not himself, who beat the youth. Umar's response is a telling example of an authentically Islamic response to issues of humanity, slavery, freedom, rulers and the ruled: 'O 'Amr! Who gives you the right to turn people into slaves, when they were born as free men from their mothers?'[119]

6. While expanding the Damascus mosque, the Umayyad caliph Walid ibn 'Abd al-Malik had a church demolished because it lay close to the mosque in the direction of the *qiblah*. Damascus Christians complained about this to the succeeding caliph 'Umar ibn 'Abd al-'Aziz. Despite the protests of local Muslims, 'Umar ibn 'Abd al-'Aziz had the extension demolished.[120] With this action he implemented the following verse concerning the protection of non-Muslim places of worship:

---

118 Muhammad Hamidullah, *The Muslim Conduct of State*, (Lahore: Sh. Muhammad Ashraf, 1968), 271. A Turkish translation is also available. See: *İslam'da Devlet İdaresi*, trans. Kemal Kuşçu, (İstanbul: Ahmed Said Matbaası: 1963), 270.

119 M. Yusuf Kandahlevi, *Hadislerle Müslümanlık*, (İstanbul: Cümle Yayınevi, 1980), vol. 2, 687.

120 Ibn Qayyim al-Jawziyyah, *Ahkām ahl al-Dhimma*, vol. 2, 683; 'Abd al-Karim Zaidan, *Ahkam al-Dhimmiyyin wa al-Musta'minin*, (Baghdad, 1382/1963), 97.

> If God did not repel some people by means of others, many monasteries, churches, synagogues, and mosques, where God's name is much invoked would have been destroyed. (*al-Hajj*, 22:40)

7. The contract signed between 'Abd al-'Aziz ibn Musa, commander of the Muslim armies in Andalusia, and the Spanish ruler Theodomiro is another example of the application of the same principle:

> Theodomiro agreed to make peace, and in return he has been given the promise and protection of Allah. As long as they abide by the agreed provisions, the properties of any Christian under his rule shall not be touched; their men, women and children shall not be killed, captured or prevented from practising their religion; their churches shall not be damaged.[121]

8. Murad II accepted the peace proposal of the despotic Serbian king Yorgi Brankovich at his own terms: he would pay 50,000 gold coins of taxes every year; he would provide military assistance to the Ottoman state upon request; and he would marry his daughter to Murad II. Sultana Mara, who lived as Murad II's wife for 12 years was never forced to convert and she continued her life as an Orthodox Christian at the Ottoman court.[122]

9. Mehmet the Conqueror gives the following assurances in the Galata treaty after the conquest of Istanbul:

> I command that they shall be entitled to keep their property, businesses, estates, cellars, gardens, mills, ships, boats and all other merchandise and I shall not contravene them. They shall keep their churches and perform their ceremonies... and no

---

121 Harbi al-Himyari, *Kitab al-Rawd al-Mitar*, (Cairo: E. Levi-Provencal, 1983), 63ff, quoted in Mehmet Özdemir, *Endülüs Müslümanları - İlim ve Kültür Tarihi*, (Ankara: Türkiye Diyanet Vakfı Yayınları, 1997), vol. 1, 35.

122 Tahsin Ünal, *Osmanlılarda Fazilet Mücadelesi*, (İstanbul: Sebil Yayınları, 1967), 49-50.

one shall force a non-Muslim to convert to Islam without his consent and they shall appoint a leader among themselves if they will.[123]

10. Catholic Hungarians and Orthodox Serbians were engaged in a sectarian war during the reign of Mehmet the Conqueror. Upon his intervention, Serbians had to decide between the rule of the Catholic Hungarians and that of the Ottomans. They sent ambassadors to both sides to ask how they would be treated. Catholics replied that Catholic churches would be built throughout the country, whereas Mehmet the Conqueror assured them that he would give the people freedom of religion and would even build churches next to the mosques. Therefore the Serbian King Brankovich chose to be under the protection of the Ottoman Empire.[124]

11. Mehmet the Conqueror had an edict written after the conquest of Bosnia on May 28, 1463, of which the original copy is currently at the Catholic Church in Milodraz. He said in the edict:

> I, Sultan Mehmet the Conqueror, announce to the whole world that these Bosnian Franciscans are under my protection by this edict and I order the following:
>
> No one shall disturb or harm the said people or their churches. They shall live in peace in my kingdom and these people, who have become immigrants, shall thrive in freedom and security. They shall return to all the lands in my kingdom and settle in their own monasteries without fear.
>
> No one from my court, from among my viziers, officers or servants, nor any of the citizens of my kingdom shall offend or harm these people.

---

123 Ahmet Akgündüz, *Osmanlı Kanunnameleri*, (İstanbul, 1990), vol. 1, 477.

124 İsmail Hami Danişmend, *İzahlı Osmanlı Kronolojisi*, (İstanbul: Doğu Kütüphanesi, 1947), vol. 1, 275; Ahmet Akgündüz, *Belgeler Gerçekleri Konuşuyor*, (İzmir, 1990), vol. 2, 10.

No one shall attack, despise or endanger the lives, properties or churches of these people. If they bring someone from other countries to my state, they shall be entitled to the same rights as well.

I swear in the name of God who created the earth and the heaven, of our Prophet Muhammad Mustafa (pbuh), of seven holy Books, of one hundred and twenty-four thousand prophets, and of the sword that I gird myself with that no one shall disobey the above orders as long as they are in my service and subject to my orders.[125]

12. Zembilli Ali Efendi and Ebussuud Efendi, who both served as chief religious officials (*Shaykh al-Islam*) in the Ottoman Empire, did not give the *fatwa* (ruling on a question of Islamic law, given by a recognised authority) to turn churches into mosques, as the Crusaders had turned mosques into churches, and the churches remained as they were.[126]

13. In the statement of protection he gave to the Armenian Patriarch of Jerusalem, Serkis III, Yavuz Sultan Selim promised that no one shall be prevented from performing their religious duties and that places of worship shall be preserved. It is underlined that all officers of the Ottoman Empire are responsible for obeying this royal decree with the following words:

> ...they shall not intervene, disturb, convert or harm any human being who is a creature of God in any way, for any reason whatsoever. Whoever shall intervene, disturb, convert or harm them shall be criminals by God who helps the sultans.[127]

---

125 Published by the Turkish Ministry of Culture to commemorate the 700th anniversary of the establishment of the Ottoman State in 1999.

126 Mehmet Niyazi, *Türk Devlet Felsefesi*, (İstanbul, 1993), 227.

127 Yavuz Ercan, *Kudus Ermeni Patrikhanesi*, (Ankara, 1988), 15-7.

14. Mahmut II: 'I differentiate the Muslims from among my subjects in the mosque, the Christians in the church and the Jews in the synagogue. I do not see the slightest difference between them. I love all of them and I treat them with justice. All of them are truly my children.'[128]

We cannot say that this tolerant approach, of which we have provided a selection of snapshots from a certain period of time, continued uninterrupted until the present. In the course of Islamic history there have been examples of interpretations and actions to the contrary. Such examples are relatively few, and it is very wrong to exaggerate them and try to ground them in religion by saying that 'Islam is a religion of the sword,' or labelling Muslims throughout history as 'barbaric.' It should not be forgotten that relationships of intolerance or oppression have always emerged from political situations of conflict and from misguided policies placing the pursuit of worldly interest above justice and obedience to God.

Did Muslims ever force others to convert to Islam in the past?

Theoretically, it is impossible for Muslims who come from a tradition that allowed Najran Christians to pray in their mosque[129] to do this. The verses in the Qur'an that underline freedom of religion, the Sunnah and the Islamic history of fifteen hundred years testify that there was no Islamic state policy to force people to convert to Islam. Some quotes from conscientious Western scholars of history support our point:

> He [the Ottoman Sultan Mehmed II] granted a toleration to the Greek Church, and also showed great civility to the patriarch of Constantinople. [130]

> (This tolerance was in sharp contrast to the intolerance and hostility existing between different Christian groups at the time. Indeed, the author goes on to discuss a letter from the Pope, Pius II, to Mehmed II, in which the Pope entreats the Sultan to convert to Christianity, gain the Pope's support for his rule over

128 Gülnihal Bozkurt, 'Osmanlı Devleti ve Gayri Müslimler,' in *Türklerde İnsani Değerler ve İnsan Hakları*, (İstanbul: Türk Kültürüne Hizmet Vakfı, 1992), vol.2, 295.

129 Ibn Hisham, *As-Sirah an-Nabawiyyah*, vol. 2, 224; Hamidullah, *İslam Peygamberi*, vol. 2, 1086.

130 Pierre Bayle, *Historical and Critical Dictionary*, (2nd ed, 1737; reprint, Routledge/Thoemmes Press, 1997), vol. 4, 55-57.

the Greeks and help the Pope and the Roman Church *against*
Greek fellow Christians who were disobedient to the Roman
religious leadership.)[131]

The Arabs under the first Caliphs... were nothing like numerous
enough to conquer and hold all the lands. Wherever they went
they gathered more soldiers to their army like a rolling snowball
[these soldiers were voluntary converts to Islam]. The Islamic
brotherhood to which they called people was a real thing, and a
new experience among Eastern nations... well established facts
dispose of the idea so widely fostered in Christian writings that
the Muslims, wherever they went, forced people to accept Islam
at the point of the sword.[132]

...the Christian Arab tribes of Northern Arabia... seem to have
become absorbed in the surrounding Muslim community by an
almost insensible process of 'peaceful penetration'; had attempts
been made to convert them by force when they first came
under Muhammadan rule, it would not have been possible for
Christians to have survived among them up to the times of the
'Abbasid caliphs. [133]

In fact, it is the Christians rather than the Muslims that deserve criticism in
this area. Christians, who were initially mercilessly persecuted in the Roman
Empire, meted out the same treatment to others, including fellow Christians,
after Christianity was accepted as the official religion of the empire. The
final comments come, again, from Western researchers:

...once given power by the succession of events following the
conversion of the Emporer Constantine, how rarely and how
feebly did the authoritative representatives of the Church resist
the temptation to world domination. The conviction that the
Church *had* to be right justified in the eyes of many not only the
defence of Europe against the Moors but the aggressive enterprises
against Islam, against Eastern Christians, and against heretics.[134]

---

131 Bayle, *Dictionary*, vol.4, 55-57.

132 L. Browne, *The Prospects of Islam*, 11-14, (cited by Abu'l Fadl Ezzati, *The Spread of Islam*, London: Saqi Books, 2002, 308.)

133 T.W Arnold, *The Spread of Islam in the World*, (Goodword Books, 1986), 50. A Turkish translation is available. See: T. W. Arnold, *İntisari İslam Tarihi*, trans. Hasan Gündüzler, (İstanbul: Akcağ Yayınları, 1982), 65-66.

134 Kathleen Bliss, *The Future of Religion*, (Pelican, 1972), 136.

We may feel certain that if Western Christians, instead of the Saracens and the Turks, had won the domination over Asia, there would be today not a trace left of the Greek Church, and that they would never have tolerated Mahometanism as the infidels have tolerated Christianity there.[135]

We [Christians] enjoy the fine advantage of being far better versed than others in the art of killing, bombarding, and exterminating the Human race.[136]

One last note: The freedom of religion and belief which was adopted in Islam from the first days of revelation was only officially recognised in mainstream Christianity in the second half of the twentieth century at the famous Second Vatican Council. Freedom of religion, which was ratified by 2308 affirmative votes against 70 negative votes on December 7, 1965, was declared in the following words:

In all his activity a man is bound to follow his conscience in order that he may come to God, the end and purpose of life. It follows that he is not to be forced to act in a manner contrary to his conscience. Nor, on the other hand, is he to be restrained from acting in accordance with his conscience, especially in matters religious. The reason is that the exercise of religion, of its very nature, consists before all else in those internal, voluntary and free acts whereby man sets the course of his life directly toward God.[137]

---

135 Pierre Bayle, cited by Arnold Toynbee, *An Historian's Approach to Religion*, (3rd ed., 1957), 205; Ezzati, *The Spread of Islam*, 28.

136 Pierre Bayle, cited by E.C Dewick, *The Christian Attitude to Other Religions*, (Cambridge University Press, 1953), 119; Ezzati, *The Spread of Islam*, 28.

137 'Declaration on Religious Freedom: Dignitatis Humanae', Vatican: the Holy See website, accessed 3rd October 2011, http://www.vatican.va/archive/hist_councils/ii_vatican_council/documents/vat-ii_decl_19651207_dignitatis-humanae_en.html

The Declaration is cited by Mehmet Aydın, *Hıristiyan Genel Konsilleri ve II. Vatikan Konsili*, (Konya: SUB Yayınları, 1991), 91f.

Under the *dhimma* treaty system, what were the rights of non-Muslim *dhimmis*?

Dhimma, which literally means indemnity, security and promise, is the temporary or permanent residency rights given to non-Muslims in the Islamic state. Such rights can be gained by treaties, birth, marriage and amnesty declared by the head of state. *Dhimma* grants security of life and property to non-Muslims, along with freedom of faith, worship, movement and work, in return for which the *dhimmis* undertake certain financial (poll tax, *jizya*) and social responsibilities.

The practice of *dhimma* treaties, first observed during the lifetime of the Prophet (pbuh), continued in all Islamic states from the Umayyads until the present. The non-Muslims who signed a *dhimma* treaty lived their lives in full freedom. The Prophet (pbuh) says:

> Whoever torments a *dhimmi* or holds him responsible for more than he can do or violates his rights or takes something from him without his consent shall be my enemy. I will avenge him on the Day of Judgement.[138]

> Whoever kills a *dhimmi* unjustly shall not smell the scent of Heaven, whose scent can be smelled from a distance of forty years of travel. [139]

> There are three things in which Muslim and unbeliever are equal. Abide by your word with whomever you had an agreement, be it a Muslim or an unbeliever. Because that agreement is made in the name of God. Visit whoever you have a kinship tie with, be it a Muslim or an unbeliever. Whoever entrusts you with something, give the entrusted to its rightful owner, be it a Muslim or an unbeliever.[140]

These norms, expressed in Prophetic *hadiths*, were systematised by scholars of Islamic law, providing *dhimmis* with full autonomy in the religious, commercial, legal, social and cultural spheres. Caliph 'Umar applied the

---

138   Abu Dawud, *Sunan Abu Dawud*, Harac wa al-Imara, hadith no. 33.

139   Al-Bukhari, *Sahih al-Bukhari*, Jizya, hadith no. 5; Abu Dawud, *Sunan Abu Dawud*, Jihad, hadith no. 165.

140   Abu Bakr Ahmad ibn al-Hussayn al-Bayhaqi, *Shu`ab al-Iman*, vol. 4, 86, hadith no. 4362.

principle of 'lex talionis' (the law of retribution: 'an eye for an eye') to the Muslims who killed *dhimmis*, saying:

> They pay us *jizya* so that their blood is like our blood and their property is like our property.[141]

The following statement of 'Umar and Sarahsi is very significant as it conveys the early Islamic approach to this issue:

> There are things advantageous to them, just as there are to us; and there are things disadvantageous to them just as there are to us. They have whatever rights we have; and they have whatever responsibilities we have because they agreed to it with the *dhimma* treaty. Their lives and properties are deemed equal to those of Muslims.[142]

The presence of non-Muslim citizens in Muslim territories who maintained the religious and national identities freely passed on by their forebears, and the survival of such historical structures as churches and synagogues should be taken as evidence of this approach. History shows that Christians did not always show the same tolerance to Muslims.

Is the *dhimma* system a way of making Muslims superior to non-Muslims? Is it applicable today?

The distinction between the Prophet's (pbuh) identity as a prophet and his religious practices, and his political practices in response to the conditions he faced as head of state should be clearly made. The example of his vision as a Prophet (pbuh) is binding upon all Muslims until the end of time, whereas the example of his actions as a head of state is not. As previously stated, we must distinguish between practical politics, legal facts and religious facts.

The *dhimma* treaty is a political agreement. It began as a practice of our Prophet (pbuh) as a head of state and can be interpreted as affirming Muslim superiority since non-Muslims constituted the minority in the Islamic state at the time that the practice was instituted. The rights/privileges granted by this treaty can even be seen as favours or concessions. Therefore, from this

---

141   Al-Jassas al-Razi, *Ahkam al-Qur'an*, vol. 1, 174-5; Fayda, *Hz. Ömer Zamanında Gayr-i Müslimler*, 166.

142   Sarahsi, *Sherh al-Siyar al-Kabeer*, vol. 3, 150.

point of view, Muslims were made superior to non-Muslims in the *dhimma* system.

Nevertheless, taking account of present day administrative, political, geographical, economic and cultural factors we must come to terms with the fact that today's Muslims are not the Muslims of the Prophet Muhammad's (pbuh) time. The *dhimma* treaty is made with non-Muslims who wish to reside in a state ruled by Muslims. They pay the Islamic state *jizya* (poll tax) in return for religious, educational and legal autonomy. They can live on the land as long as they abide by the treaty.

In today's legal-administrative systems, obtaining a visa or permanent right of residence is the equivalent of the *dhimma* system. When obtaining a visa a foreign national is required to follow a set procedure, complete forms, attend an interview and often pay a fee to obtain a visa for entry into another country where he can stay for a limited period of time. During his stay, his rights are restricted – for example he cannot apply for certain benefits and he needs to register his address with the police. The current immigration law in the United States, for all its imperfections, very accurately reflects the *dhimma* system in Islam.

The *dhimma* system is best understood as a political system helpful for maintaining peace and stability in the early period of Islam in Muslim-majority states. In this era of nation-states, when religion and political allegiance are no longer inextricably linked, the *dhimma* system in its original form, in which Muslims and non-Muslims have a different status and relationship to the state, is not applicable.

Conclusion

This book, on the basis of Islamic sources, commends dialogue to its Muslim readers. As we explained in Chapter 1, by dialogue we mean meaningful interaction and exchange between people of different groups (social, cultural, political and religious) who come together through various kinds of conversations or activities with a view to increased understanding. As discussed in that chapter, dialogue, at its most profound, can be an enlightening and even transformative human experience, which can foster a deep understanding and appreciation of one's fellow human beings without undermining one's own religious and cultural identity. The mutual understanding that any sincere dialogue promotes can have great social value in inter-group relations as well as considerable personal benefits. However, our main concern in this book has been to demonstrate that, aside from the benefits that it may bring, dialogue claims the attention of Muslims because it is a truly Islamic mindset, outlook and practice.

We argued in Chapter 1 that, apart from any external benefits, it may have, dialogue is an inherently valuable expression of our God-given human nature, our *fitra*. We were created for engagement with our Creator, as we are told in the Qur'an, *al-Dhariyat,* 51:56: I created jinn and mankind only to worship Me.

Our spiritual make-up is fitted for worship, for engagement with God. Similarly, our nature, from our mental and physiological capacities for speech to our faces' capacity for subtle expression, fits us for engagement with our fellow human beings. *Surat an-Nahl* explains that in the grains and fruits of the earth and in the motion of sun, moon and stars there are 'Signs for men who are wise.' Those who are wise should surely not neglect the signs embedded in the creation of the human person, which guide us towards communication with all those who share our humanity.

The diversity of humanity is surely another sign. It guides us towards engagement with people different from ourselves. This *ayah* (sign) in creation is underlined by *ayat* (verses) in the Qur'an highlighting diversity and indicating the appropriate response to it, as in *al-Hujurat,* 49:13:

> People, we created you all from a single man and a single woman,
> and made you into races and tribes so that you should get to
> know one another. In God's eyes, the most honoured of you are
> the ones most mindful of Him: God is all knowing, all aware.

A range of *ayat* (verses) of the Qur'an, which we considered in Chapter
2, urge Muslims to foster just, compassionate, respectful relations with the
People of the Book and with those of other faiths and cultures. Verses such
as *al-Baqara,* 2:256, 'there is no compulsion in religion', establish freedom
of religion. The Sunnah, the 'beautiful pattern' (*al-Ahzab,* 33:21) of the
Prophet's (pbuh) conduct, contains ample examples of fair, generous dealings
with diverse groups, and of friendly relations with groups and individuals
of other faiths whose conduct made such relations feasible. Islamic history
provides numerous examples of efforts made to promote peaceful, just and
respectful inter-group relations and to protect the religious rights and the
dignity of other faith groups. Thus the Qur'an, the Sunnah and Islamic
history all lend compelling support to the practice of positive, meaningful
engagement with people of different faiths and cultures.

In the course of this book we have discussed passages from Islamic sources
which, at a glance, appear to contradict the material supporting dialogue. Verses
of the Qur'an which warn against taking 'Jews and Christians' as friends, or
which speak of killing unbelievers, and reports of the Prophet (pbuh) fighting
and punishing Jewish tribes require careful consideration. Our position is that
none of this material is opposed to dialogue in general if properly understood.
To be true to the sources, and to understand the eternally valid Qur'an and
the conduct of the Prophet (pbuh) we need to expend intellectual effort
and to take a holistic view of the Qur'an and of the Sunnah. Considering
a particular verse or tradition in isolation will not facilitate an accurate
understanding of its meaning. We must instead ponder the meaning of a verse
or *hadith* in the context of the whole Qur'an, or the whole Sunnah, and of
the historical circumstances of the verse's revelation or the Prophet's (pbuh)
action or statement. In doing so we reach an understanding which respects the
coherence of the source and which has a firmer claim to accuracy.[143]

---

143 Similarly, when we consider the decision or opinion of historical Islamic scholars, we must consider the historical context in
   which it was made and its relation to relevant decisions and opinions from other reputable scholars in different contexts in
   order to ascertain its relevance for our time and circumstances.

For instance, consideration of the occasions of revelation of verses on killing unbelievers, and reflection on their relationship to verses commanding tolerance and moderation, shows us that the subject of these verses is not unbelievers per se but hostile combatant unbelievers in a state of war. The verses are eternally valid, but their scope is limited. They govern our conduct towards a restricted group in a restricted set of circumstances. They would govern the conduct of a modern Muslim caught up in a conflict with non-Muslims engaged in attacking them. This is not to say that they would govern the behaviour of a modern Muslim in a state of peace, living alongside people of a different faith.

The default position of the Qur'an is one of peace. The default attitude of the Qur'an and the Sunnah, and accordingly of faithful Muslims, is one of respect and generosity towards those of different faiths and cultures.

It is our belief that the *practice* of intercultural and interfaith dialogue engaged in on the basis of Islamic inspiration sheds light on the proper relationship of a Muslim to those of different faiths and cultures. Because it is a natural expression of our God-given nature, and a response to the commands of God in Islamic sources, it can also enrich a person's experience as a human being and as a Muslim. In addition, it can have great external benefits, fostering respect, trust and solidarity between different religious and cultural groups and allowing them to collaborate in addressing shared problems. In the contexts of our increasingly diverse societies, of the constant intercultural contact of the global village and of the social, political, moral and environmental challenges faced by humanity in the modern world, dialogue is invaluable. We commend dialogue to you as an indispensable element of faithful Muslim life, on the basis of Islamic sources, rather than as a means to external benefits. Nevertheless, we hope and trust that by engaging in dialogue you will reap all kinds of benefits.

As we conclude our discussion, we note once more that in commending dialogue we are not necessarily commending *theological* interaction and exchange. In defining dialogue as meaningful interaction between different groups we have left open the question of the topics of conversation broached in that interaction. Dialogue (including interfaith dialogue) does not require readiness to discuss theological matters with people of other religions; it requires only an openness to diversity as a source of blessing, and to positive and constructive engagement with people of different backgrounds and outlooks.

It is worth making this point because, for whatever reason, a number of people, Muslim or otherwise, might be uncomfortable with theological dialogue and prefer not to take part in such conversation. This does not impede the point made in this book in the slightest, since we are not referring to theological discussion when referring to dialogue. What we are arguing is that faithful Muslims should have an attitude of openness to intercultural dialogue that manifests itself in day-to-day life, from making an effort to be friendlier with your neighbour to taking a more active interest in promoting cohesiveness in wider society.

To those readers who disagree with elements of our argument, or even with the whole thrust of the book, we end by suggesting that the best way to express your disagreement is by engaging in dialogue, asking to be understood while making an effort to understand. If we wish to understand each other's positions, dialogue is inescapable, and it is the only way we can ever really learn from each other.

Glossary of Terms

ahad – (of a **hadith**) (lit. single) reported by only one, two, or three different narrators of the same generation (*see also* **mashhur**; **mutawatir**)

aman – security

amr bi-l-ma'ruf wa-nahy 'ani l-munkar – bidding to the good and forbidding from the evil

asbab (*sing.* sabab) al-nuzul – occasions of the sending down, revelation of the Qur'an

ayah (*pl.* ayat) – sign(s), verse(s) of the Qur'an; natural phenomenon/a, intelligible as sign(s) of the Creator

dar al-harb – domain of war; territory beyond the rule of Islam

dar al-Islam – domain of peace; territory within the rule of Islam

da'wah – call, invitation to Islam

dhimma – obligation/treaty of protection with non-Muslims under the rule of Islam

dhimmi – person subject to a **dhimma** (q.v.)

fard – mandatory religious obligation; duty

fatwa – ruling on a question of Islamic law, given by a recognised authority

fiqh – jurisprudence

fitna – trial, tribulation (contextually defined, e.g. religious persecution, civil war)

fitra – innate disposition

hadith – saying of the Prophet Muhammad (pbuh)

ijtihad – interpretation of the teaching of the Qur'an and Sunnah; the process of exerting conscience and reason to derive a scholarly opinion or legal ruling from the sources

iman – faith, conviction

irshad – guidance, direction

irtidad – turning back, reverting (apostasising) from Islam

jahiliyya – (lit. ignorance) pre-Islamic era, pre-Islamic attitudes

jihad – effort, endeavour (physical, mental or spiritual)

jizya – poll tax imposed on people subject to the **dhimma** (q.v.)

kafir – unbeliever

kharaj – land tax

madhhab – doctrine or school of law

mansukh – abrogated (*see* **nasikh**)

mashhur – (of a **hadith**) (lit. well-known) reported by several narrators and transmitted through several chains of narration, though through fewer chains than a **hadith** which is **mutawatir** (*see also* **ahad**; **mutawatir**)

mufassir – exegete, interpreter of the Qur'an (*see* **tafsir**)

muhkam – (of Qur'anic verses) explicit, embodying an unambiguous command or exhortation (*see also* **mujmal**; **muqayyad**; **mutashabih**; **mutlaq**)

mujahid – person engaged in **jihad** (q.v.)

mujmal – (of Qur'anic verses) ambiguous, composite (*see also* **muhkam**; **muqayyad**; **mutashabih**; **mutlaq**)

munafiq – hypocrite (person outwardly professing Islam, while secretly opposing and conspiring against the Muslims)

muqayyad – (of Qur'anic verses) restricted (*see also* **muhkam**; **mujmal**; **mutashabih**; **mutlaq**)

murtad – one who has quit Islam, apostate (*see* **irtidad**)

mushriq – (lit. associator, who associates other gods with God) polytheist or idolater

mutashabih – (of Qur'anic verses) allegorical, whose precise referents are known only to God (*see also* **muhkam**; **mujmal**; **muqayyad**; **mutlaq**)

mutawatir – (lit. reported by many from many) reported by many narrators in the same generation and passed down through many chains of narration (*see also* **ahad**; **mashhur**)

mutlaq – (of Qur'anic verses) absolute (*see also* **muhkam**; **mujmal**; **muqayyad**; **mutashabih**)

nafs – self or soul

al-nafs al-ammara – evil-commanding self

nas – people, humankind

nasiha – advice, counsel

nasikh – abrogating (*see* **mansukh**)

al-qawl al-layyin – mild-mannered discourse

sabab – *see* **asbab**

Sunnah – the example, precepts and practice of the Prophet Muhammad (pbuh)

Sunnatullah – the norms of God's creation

surah – chapter of the Qur'an

tabligh – presenting, preaching Islam

tafsir – exegesis, interpretation of the Qur'an (*see* **mufassir**)

taqwa – heedfulness, wariness of God; piety, God-fearing

ummah – community, society identified by a way of life; the supranational community of Muslims

wali – friend; confidant

wa'z – preaching, addressing the heart

Bibliography

Abdul Baqi, Muhammad Fuad. *Al Mujam el Mofahras Li Alfaz al Qur'an al Kareem.* Damascus: Dar Al Hadeeth.

Abu Ya'la al-Mawsili, Ahmad b. 'Ali b. al-Muthanna. *Al-Musnad.*

Abu Yusuf, Yaqub ibn Ibrahim. *Kitab al-Kharaj.* Cairo, 1962.

Akgündüz, Ahmet. *Belgeler Gerçekleri Konuşuyor.* İzmir, 1990.

Akgündüz, Ahmet. *Osmanlı Kanunnameleri.* İstanbul, 1990.

Al-Aqqad, Abbas Mahmud. *Majmu'at al-Abqariyat al-Islamiyah.* Beirut, 1968.

Al-Baidawi, 'Abdallah b. 'Umar. *Anwar al-Tanzeel.* Cairo, 1330/1912.

Al-Bajuri, Ibrahim. *Hashiya al-Bajuri ala Sharh ibn Qasim.*

Al-Baladhuri, Ahmad b. Yahya. *Futuh al Buldan.* Translated by Mustafa Fayda. Ankara, 1987.

Al-Baladhuri, Ahmad b. Yahya. *Kitab Futuh al-Buldan.* Beirut: Dar al-Ma'arif, 1987.

Al-Bayhaqi, Abu Bakr Ahmad ibn al-Hussayn. *Shu`ab al-Iman.*

Al-Bukhari, Muhammad ibn Isma'il. *Al-Adab al-Mufrad.*

Al-Bukhari, Muhammad ibn Isma'il. *Sahih al-Bukhari.*

Al-Darimi, `Abd Allah ibn `Abd al-Rahman, *Sunan al-Darimi.*

Al-Fairuzabadi, Abu al-Tahir ibn Ibrahim Majd al-Din. *Al-Qamus al-Muhit.*

Al-Himyari, Harbi. *Kitab al-Rawd al-Mitar.* Cairo: E. Levi-Provencal, 1983.

Al-'Ijlouni, Isma'il b. Muhammad. *Kashf al-Khafa'*. Cairo.

Al-Isfahani, al-Raghib. *Al-Mufradat fi Gharib al-Qur'an*. İstanbul: Kahraman Yayınları, 1986.

Al-Jassas al-Razi, Abu Bakr. *Ahkam al-Qur'an*.

Al-Jurjani. *Kitab at-Ta'rifat*. Beirut: Matkabat Lebanon, 1978.

Al-Muttagi, Ali. *Kanz al-Ummal*.

Al-Nasa'i, Ahmad ibn Shu`ayb ibn Alī ibn Sīnān Abū `Abd ar-Rahmān. *Sunan an-Nasa'i*.

Al-Nisaburi, Al-Hasan ibn Muhammad. *Ghara'ib al-Qur'an wa-Ragha-ib al-Furqan*. Beirut: Dar al-Ma'rifa,1992.

Al-Qari, Ali ibn Sultan. *Asrar al-Marfu'ah fi Akhbar al-Mawdu'ah*.

Al-Razi, Fakhr al-Din. *Al-Tafsir al-Kabir*. Beirut: Dar Ihya al-Turath al'Arabi.

Al-Shafi'i, Abu Abdullah Muhammad ibn Idris. *Kitab al-Umm*. Beirut: Dar al-Fikr, 1983.

Al-Sijistani, Abu Dawud. *Sunan Abu Dawud*.

Al-Suyuti, Abu al-Fadl 'Abd al-Rahman ibn Abi Bakr Jalal al-Din. *Al-Itqan fi 'Ulum al-Qur'an*. Cairo: Halabi, 1354/1935.

Al-Suyuti, Abu al-Fadl 'Abd al-Rahman ibn Abi Bakr Jalal al-Din. *Asbab al-Nuzul*. Cairo: Dar al-Manar.

Al-Tabari, Abu Ja'far Muhammad ibn Jarir. *Annals of the Prophets and Kings*. Brill, 2010.

Al-Tabari, Abu Ja'far Muhammad ibn Jarir. *Jami al-Bayan fi Ta'wil al-Qur'an*. Cairo: Dar al-Maarif.

Al-Tabari, Abu Ja'far Muhammad ibn Jarir. *Tarikh al-Tabari*. Cairo: Muhammad Abu'l Fazl, 1970.

Al Tirmidhi, Muhammad b. 'Isa. *Jami al-Tirmidhi.*

'Amara, Muhammad. *Al-Islam wa Huquq al-Insan: Darurat...la Huquq (Islam and Human Rights: Necessities...not Rights).* Kuwait: 'Alam al-Ma'rifa, 1405/1985.

'Amara, Muhammad. *Islam and Human Rights: Requisite Necessities Rather than Mere Rights.* Publications of the Islamic Educational, Scientific and Cultural Organization, 1996.

'Amara (/Umara), Muhammad. *İslam ve İnsan Hakları.* Translated by Asım Kanar. İstanbul: Denge Yayınları, 1992.

Arnold, T.W. *Intisari İslam Tarihi.* Translated by Hasan Gündüzler. İstanbul: Akcağ Yayınları, 1982.

Arnold, T.W. *The Spread of Islam in the World.* Goodword Books, 1986.

Atalay, Orhan. *Doğu-Batı Kaynaklarında Birlikte Yaşama.* İstanbul: Gazeteciler ve Yazarlar Vakfı Yayınları, 1999.

Aydın, Mehmet. *Hıristiyan Genel Konsilleri ve II. Vatikan Konsili.* Konya: SUB Yayınları, 1991.

Bayle, Pierre. *Historical and Critical Dictionary.* 2nd edition, 1737. Reprint, Routledge/Thoemmes Press, 1997.

Bliss, Kathleen. *The Future of Religion.* Pelican, 1972.

Bohm, David. *On Dialogue.* Abingdon, Oxon: Routledge, 2004.

Bohm, David, Donald Factor and Peter Garrett. *Dialogue- A Proposal.* 1991. http://www.david-bohm.net/dialogue/dialogue_proposal.html.

Bozkurt, Gülnihal. 'Osmanlı Devleti ve Gayri Müslimler.' In *Türklerde İnsani Değerler ve İnsan Hakları.* İstanbul: Türk Kültürüne Hizmet Vakfı,1992.

Buber, Martin. *I and Thou.* New York: Simon and Schuster, 1971.

Bulaç, Ali. 'Cihat.' *Yeni Ümit,* 63(2004).

Cemil, Haşim. 'al-Salaam fi al-Islam.' *Risala al-Islamiyya* 63-64.

Committee appointed by Turkey's National Directorate of Religious Affairs (Diyanet). *Kur'an Yolu.* Ankara: Diyanet İşleri Baskanlığı Yayınları, 2003.

Danişmend, İsmail Hami. *İzahlı Osmanlı Kronolojisi.* İstanbul: Doğu Kütüphanesi, 1947.

Dewick, E.C. *The Christian Attitude to Other Religions.* Cambridge University Press, 1953.

Elmalılı, Muhammed Hamdi Yazır. *Hak Dini Kur'an Dili.* İstanbul: Zehraveyn Yayınları, 1992.

Ercan, Yavuz. *Kudus Ermeni Patrikhanesi.* Ankara, 1988.

Erdal, Mesut. 'Kur'an'da Fitne Kavramı Üzerine Düşünceler.' *DUIFD* 1(1991).

Eren, Sadi. *Cihad ve Savaş.* İstanbul: Nesil, 1996.

Ezzati, Abu'l-Fadl. *İslamın Yayılış Tarihine Giriş.* Translated by Cahid Koytak. İstanbul: İnsan Yayınları, 1984.

Ezzati, Abu'l-Fadl. *The Spread of Islam.* London: Saqi Books, 2002.

Fayda, Mustafa. *Hz. Ömer Zamanında Gayr-i Müslimler.* İstanbul: Marmara Üniversitesi İlahiyat Fakültesi Yayınları, 1989.

Garlow, James. *A Christian's Response to Islam.* Oklahoma: RiverOak Publishing, 2002.

Gülen, M. Fethullah. *Asrın Getirdiüi Tereddütler.* İzmir: Nil Yayınları, 1998.

Gülen, M Fethullah. *Gurbet Ufukları.* İstanbul: Gazeteciler ve Yazarlar Vakfı, 2004.

Gülen, M. Fethullah. *İ'la-yi Kelimetullah veya Cihad.* İzmir: Nil Yayınları, 1997.

Güner, Osman. *Resulullah'ın Ehli Kitapla Münasebetleri.* Ankara: Fecr Yayıncılık, 1997.

Güneş, Ahmet. 'Views on the Rules of the War.' In *Terror and Suicide Attacks: an Islamic Perspective*, edited by Ergün Çapan, 120-131. New Jersey: The Light Inc, 2004.

Hamidullah, Muhammad. *Hz. Peygamber'in Savaşları*. Translated by Salih Tuğ. İstanbul: Yağmur Yayınları, 2002.

Hamidullah, Muhammad. *İslam Peygamberi*. Translated by Salih Tuğ. İstanbul: İrfan Yayınları, 2004.

Hamidullah, Muhammad. *İslam'da Devlet İdaresi*. Translated by Kemal Kuşçu. İstanbul: Ahmed Said Matbaası, 1963.

Hamidullah, Muhammad. *Mecmua Wasaiq al-Siyasiyye*. Beirut: Dar al-Nafais, 1985.

Hamidullah, Muhammad. *The Battlefields of the Prophet Muhamma*. Luton: Apex Books, 1975.

Hamidullah, Muhammad. *The Life and Work of the Founder of Islam*. Luton: Apex Books Concern, 1975.

Hamidullah, Muhammad. *The Muslim Conduct of State*. Lahore: Sh. Muhammad Ashraf, 1968.

Ibn Abi Shayba, Abu Bakr al-'Abasi. *Al-Musannaf*.

Ibn Abidin, Muhammad Amin. *Radd al-Muhtar ala ad-Dur al-Mukhtar*. Dar Al Marefa, [2004].

Ibn al-Hajjaj, Muslim. *Sahih Muslim*.

Ibn al-Human, Kamaluddin M. *Fath al-Qadir*. Mısr, 1356/1937.

Ibn Hanbal al-Shaybani, Abu `Abd Allah Ahmad ibn Muhammad. *Musnad*.

Ibn Hisham, Abu Muhammad 'Abd al-Malik. *As-Sirah an-Nabawiyyah*. Cairo, 1413/1992.

Ibn Hisham, Abu Muhammad 'Abd al-Malik. *As-Sirah an-Nabawiyyah*. Dar al-Turas al-Arabiyya, 1971.

Ibn Kathir, Abu al-Fida Ishmai'l. *Tafsir al-Qur'an al-Azim*. Beirut, 1961.

Ibn Majah, Abu 'Abdillah Muhammad ibn Yazid. *Sunan ibn Majah.*

Ibn Manzur, Muhammad ibn Mukarram ibn Ali ibn Ahmad. *Lisan al-Arab.* Beirut: Dar Sadr.

Ibn Qayyim al-Jawziyyah (Muhammad ibn Abu Bakr). *Ahkām ahl al-Dhimma.* Damascus: Matbaa Jami'a Dimashq, 1381/1961.

Ibn Qayyim al-Jawziyyah (Muhammad ibn Abu Bakr). *Zad al Maad.* Cairo: Muhammad Hamid al-Faqqi, 1373/1953.

Ibn Sa'd, Muhammad. *Kitab Tabaqat al-Kubra*. Beirut, [c.1960].

Kandahlevi, M. Yusuf. *Hadislerle Müslümanlık*. İstanbul: Cümle Yayınevi, 1980.

Lings, Martin. *Muhammad: His Life Based on the Earliest Sources*. New York: Inner Traditions, 1987.

Mahzun, Muhammad. *Tahqiq Mawaqif al-Sahaba fi al-Fitna: min Riwayat al-Iman al-Tabari wa al-Muhaddithin*. Riyadh, 1994.

Merginani, Burhanuddin. *Al-Hidaya Sharhu Bidayati'l-Mubtadi*. İstanbul, 1986.

Miras, Kamil. *Tecrid-i Sarih Muhtasarı, Sahih-i Buhari Tercemesi*. Ankara: Başbakanlık Basımevi, 1966.

Niyazi, Mehmet. *Türk Devlet Felsefesi*. İstanbul, 1993.

Nursi, Bediüzzaman Said. *Kaynaklı, İndeksli, Lügatlı Risale-i Nur Külliyatı*. İstanbul: Nesil Basım Yayın, 1996.

Nursi, Bediüzzaman Said. *Münazarat*. İstanbul: Yeni Asya Yayınevi, 1998.

Nursi, Bediüzzaman Said. *The Words*. New Jersey: The Light, 2005.

Nursi, Bediüzzaman Said. *The Words*. Translated by Şükran Vahide. İstanbul: Sözler Publications, 1993.

Özdemir, Mehmet. *Endülüs Müslümanları - İlim ve Kültür Tarihi*. Ankara: Türkiye Diyanet Vakfı Yayınları, 1997.

Özel, Ahmet. 'Cihat.' In *DİA (Diyanet İslam Ansiklopedisi)*. İstanbul, [1995].

Qutb, Sayyid. *In the Shade of the Qur'an, Fi Zilal al Qur'an*. Translated and edited by Abil Salahi. Markfield: The Islamic Foundation, 2001.

Republic of Turkey's Ministry for Foreign Affairs. 'Armenians in Ottoman Bureaucracy.' Accessed 6th October 2011. http://www.mfa.gov.tr/armenians-in-ottoman-bureaucracy.en.mfa

Saeed, Abdullah and Hassan Saeed. *Freedom of Religion, Apostasy and Islam*. Ashgate, 2004.

Sarahsi, Muhammed b. Ahmad. *Sherh al-Siyar al-Kabeer*. Beirut, 1997.

Schacht, Joseph. *An Introduction to Islamic Law*. Oxford: Oxford University Press, 1964.

The Constitution Society. 'Full Text of the Madina Charter.' Accessed 10th November, 2011. http://www.constitution.org/cons/medina/macharter.htm

The Constitution Society. 'The Medina Charter.' Accessed 30th May, 2011. http://www.constitution.org/cons/medina/con_medina.htm. (The text is taken from A. Guillaume, *The Life of Muhammad* — A Translation of Ishaq's Sirat Rasul Allah, (Oxford University Press, Karachi, 1955), 231-233. Numbering added.)

Toynbee, Arnold. *An Historian's Approach to Religion*. 3rd edition, 1957.

Ünal, Tahsin. *Osmanlılarda Fazilet Mücadelesi*. İstanbul: Sebil Yayınları, 1967.

United Nations. 'The Universal Declaration of Human Rights.' Accessed 30th May 2011. http://www.un.org/en/documents/udhr/.

Vatican: the Holy See. 'Declaration on Religious Freedom: Dignitatis Humanae.' Accessed 3rd October 2011. http://www.vatican.va/archive/hist_councils/ii_vatican_council/documents/vat-ii_decl_19651207_dignitatis-humanae_en.html

Yankelovich, Daniel. *The Magic of Dialogue*. New York: Simon and Schuster, 1999.

Yavuz, Yunus Vehbi. *İslam'da Düşünce ve İnanç Özgürlüğü*. İstanbul: Sahaflar Yayıncılık, 1994.

Yıldırım, Suat. *Kuran-ı Hakim Ve Açıklamalı Meali*. İstanbul: Define Yayınları, 1998.

Zaidan, 'Abd al-Karim, *Ahkam al-Dhimmiyyin wa al-Mustaminin*. Baghdad, 1382/1963.

Appendices

Appendix I: The Medina Charter

From The Constitution Society website, http://www.constitution.org/cons/medina/con_medina.htm. Accessed 30th May, 2011.

The text is taken from A. Guillaume, *The Life of Muhammad — A Translation of Ishaq's Sirat Rasul Allah*, (Oxford University Press, Karachi, 1955), 231-233. Numbering added.

THE MEDINA CHARTER

622 C.E.

In the name of God the Compassionate, the Merciful.

(1) This is a document from Muhammad the prophet (governing the relations) between the believers and Muslims of Quraysh and Yathrib, and those who followed them and joined them and labored with them.

(2) They are one community (*ummah*) to the exclusion of all men.

(3) The Quraysh emigrants according to their present custom shall pay the bloodwit within their number and shall redeem their prisoners with the kindness and justice common among believers.

(4-8) The B. 'Auf according to their present custom shall pay the bloodwit they paid in heatheism; every section shall redeem its prisoners with the kindness and justice common among believers. The B. Sa'ida, the B. 'l-Harith, and the B. Jusham, and the B. al-Najjar likewise.

(9-11) The B. 'Amr b. 'Auf, the B. al-Nabit and the B. al-'Aus likewise.

(12)(a) Believers shall not leave anyone destitute among them by not paying his redemption money or bloodwit in kindness.

(12)(b) A believer shall not take as an ally the freedman of another Muslim against him.

(13) The God-fearing believers shall be against the rebellious or him who seeks to spread injustice, or sin or animosity, or corruption between believers; the hand of every man shall be against him even if he be a son of one of them.

(14) A believer shall not slay a believer for the sake of an unbeliever, nor shall he aid an unbeliever against a believer.

(15) God's protection is one, the least of them may give protection to a stranger on their behalf. Believers are friends one to the other to the exclusion of outsiders.

(16) To the Jew who follows us belong help and equality. He shall not be wronged nor shall his enemies be aided.

(17) The peace of the believers is indivisible. No separate peace shall be made when believers are fighting in the way of God. Conditions must be fair and equitable to all.

(18) In every foray a rider must take another behind him.

(19) The believers must avenge the blood of one another shed in the way of God.

(20)(a) The God-fearing believers enjoy the best and most upright guidance.

(20)(b) No polytheist shall take the property of person of Quraysh under his protection nor shall he intervene against a believer.

(21) Whoever is convicted of killing a believer without good reason shall be subject to retaliation unless the next of kin is satisfied (with blood-money), and the believers shall be against him as one man, and they are bound to take action against him.

(22) It shall not be lawful to a believer who holds by what is in this document and believes in God and the last day to help an evil-doer or to shelter him. The curse of God and His anger on the day of resurrection will be upon him if he does, and neither repentance nor ransom will be received from him.

(23) Whenever you differ about a matter it must be referred to God and to Muhammad.

(24) The Jews shall contribute to the cost of war so long as they are fighting alongside the believers.

(25) The Jews of the B. 'Auf are one community with the believers (the Jews have their religion and the Muslims have theirs), their freedmen and their persons except those who behave unjustly and sinfully, for they hurt but themselves and their families.

(26-35) The same applies to the Jews of the B. al-Najjar, B. al-Harith, B. Sai ida, B. Jusham, B. al-Aus, B. Tha'laba, and the Jafna, a clan of the Tha'laba and the B. al-Shutayba. Loyalty is a protection against treachery. The freedmen of Tha 'laba are as themselves. The close friends of the Jews are as themselves.

(36) None of them shall go out to war save the permission of Muhammad, but he shall not be prevented from taking revenge for a wound. He who slays a man without warning slays himself and his household, unless it be one who has wronged him, for God will accept that.

(37) The Jews must bear their expenses and the Muslims their expenses. Each must help the other against anyone who attacks the people of this document. They must seek mutual advice and consultation, and loyalty is a protection against treachery. A man is not liable for his ally's misdeeds. The wronged must be helped.

(38) The Jews must pay with the believers so long as war lasts.

(39) Yathrib shall be a sanctuary for the people of this document.

(40) A stranger under protection shall be as his host doing no harm and committing no crime.

(41) A woman shall only be given protection with the consent of her family.

(42) If any dispute or controversy likely to cause trouble should arise it must be referred to God and to Muhammad the apostle of God. God accepts what is nearest to piety and goodness in this document.

(43) Quraysh and their helpers shall not be given protection.

(44) The contracting parties are bound to help one another against any attack on Yathrib.

(45)(a) If they are called to make peace and maintain it they must do so; and if they make a similar demand on the Muslims it must be carried out except in the case of a holy war.

(45)(b) Every one shall have his portion from the side to which he belongs.

(46) The Jews of al-Aus, their freedmen and themselves have the same standing with the people of this document in purely loyalty from the people of this document. Loyalty is a protection against treachery. He who acquires aught acquires it for himself. God approves of this document.

(47) This deed will not protect the unjust and the sinner. The man who goes forth to fight and the man who stays at home in the city is safe unless he has been unjust and sinned. God is the protector of the good and God-fearing man and Muhammad is the apostle of God.

Appendix 2: Verses from the Qur'an that relate to dialogue

The translation used is that of M.A.S Abdel Haleem (Oxford: Oxford University Press: 2010)

(Footnotes from the 2010 edition are included here)

Other translations, including Yusuf Ali's widely used translation, can be found online at http://quran.com.

Signs in Creation

People, we created you all from a single man and a single woman, and made you into races and tribes so that you should get to know one another.[144] In God's eyes, the most honoured of you are the ones most mindful of Him: God is all knowing, all aware.[145] *(Al-Hujurat, 49:13)*

We have honoured the children of Adam and carried them by land and sea; We have provided good sustenance for them and favoured them specially above many of those We have created. *(Al-Isra', 17:70)*

Another of His signs is the creation of the heavens and earth, and the diversity of your languages and colours. There truly are signs in this for those who know. *(Al-Rum, 30:22)*

I created jinn and mankind only to worship Me. *(Al-Dhariyat, 51:56)*

Diversity of belief and freedom of religion

Say, 'Now the truth has come from your Lord: let those who wish to believe in it do so, and let those who wish to reject it do so.' *(Al-Kahf, 18:29)*

There is no compulsion in religion. *(Al-Baqara, 2:256)*

Had your Lord willed, all the people on earth would have believed. So can you [Prophet] compel people to believe? *(Yunus, 10:99)*

---

144 As relatives from the same origin.

145 Of people's true worth and the thoughts they harbour.

If God had so pleased, He could have made them a single community. (*Al-Shura*, 42:8)

If God so willed, He would have made you all one people. (*Al-Nahl*, 16:93)

If your Lord had pleased, He would have made all people a single community, but they continue to have their differences – except those on whom your Lord has mercy – for He created them to be this way. (*Hud*, 11:118-119)

We have assigned a law and a path to each of you. If God had so willed, He would have made you one community, but He wanted to test you through that which He has given you, so race to do good: you will all return to God and He will make clear to you the matters you differed about. (*Al-Ma'ida*, 5:48)

Each community has its own direction to which it turns: race to do good deeds and wherever you are, God will bring you together.[146] God has power to do everything. (*Al-Baqara*, 2:148)

The People of the Book

[Believers], argue only in the best way with the People of the Book, except with those of them who act unjustly. Say, 'We believe in what was revealed to us and in what was revealed to you; our God and your God is one [and the same]; we are devoted to Him.' (*Al-'Ankabut*, 29:46)

The [Muslim] believers, the Jews, the Christians, and the Sabians[147] – those who believe in God and the Last Day and do good – will have their rewards with their Lord. No fear for them, nor will they grieve. (*Al-Baqara*, 2:62)

For the [Muslim] believers, the Jews, the Sabians,[148] and the Christians – those who believe in God and the Last Day and do good deeds – there is no fear: they will not grieve. (*Al-Ma'ida*, 5:69)

---

146 On the Day of Judgement.

147 The Sabians were a monotheistic religious community. See M. Asad, *The Message of the Qur'an* (Gibraltar: Dar al- Andalus, 1997), 40 n.49.

148 See note to 2:62.

As for the believers, those who follow the Jewish faith, the Sabians,[149] the Christians, the Magians,[150] and the idolaters, God will judge between them on the Day of Resurrection; God witnesses all things. *(Al-Hajj, 22:17)*

Some of the People of the Book believe in God, in what has been sent down to you and in what was sent down to them: humbling themselves before God, they would never sell God's revelation for a small price. These people will have their rewards with their Lord: God is swift in reckoning. *(Al-'Imran, 3:199)*

Say, 'People of the Book, let us arrive at a statement that is common to us all: we worship God alone, we ascribe no partner to Him, and none of us takes others beside God as lords.' *(Al-'Imran, 3:64)*

But they are not all alike. There are some among the People of the Book who are upright, who recite God's revelations during the night, who bow down in worship, who believe in God and the Last Day, who order what is right and forbid what is wrong, who are quick to do good deeds. These people are among the righteous and they will not be denied [the reward] for whatever good deeds they do: God knows exactly who is conscious of Him. *(Al-'Imran, 3:113-115)*

You are sure to find that the closest in affection towards the believers are those who say, 'We are Christians,' for there are among them people devoted to learning and ascetics.[151] These people are not given to arrogance. *(Al-Ma'ida, 5:82)*

Prophet Muhammad (pbuh) and the other prophets

The Messenger believes in what has been sent down to him from his Lord, as do the faithful. They all believe in God, His angels, His scriptures, and His messengers. 'We make no distinction between any of His messengers,' they say, 'We hear and obey. Grant us your forgiveness, our Lord. To You we all return!' *(Al-Baqara, 2:285)*

---

149 See note to 2:62.

150 Followers of an ancient Persian and Median religion, based on monotheism, identified with Zoroastrians.

151 Most translators render these as 'priests and monks', which are their modern meanings, not the etymological senses of the words (al-Raghib, *Mufradat*).

Zachariah, John, Jesus, and Elijah – every one of them was righteous. *(Al-An'am, 6:85)*

Say [Muhammad], 'We [Muslims] believe in God and in what has been sent down to us and to Abraham, Ishmael, Isaac, Jacob, and the Tribes. We believe in what has been given to Moses, Jesus, and the prophets from their Lord. We do not make a distinction between any of them. It is to Him that we devote ourselves.' *(Al-'Imran, 3:84)*

We have sent revelation to you [Muhammad] as We did to Noah and the prophets after him, to Abraham, Ishmael, Isaac, Jacob, and the Tribes, to Jesus, Job, Jonah, Aaron, and Solomon – to David We gave the book [of Psalms]. *(Al-Nisa', 4:163)*

Kindness, mercy and doing good

It was only as a mercy that we sent you [Prophet] to all people.[152] *(Al-Anbiya', 21:107)*

And He does not forbid you to deal kindly and justly with anyone who has not fought you for your faith or driven you out of your homes: God loves the just. *(Al-Mumtahana, 60:8)*

Be tolerant and command what is right: pay no attention to foolish people. *(Al-A'raf, 7:199)*

But if you desire God, His Messenger, and the Final Home, then remember that God has prepared great rewards for those of you who do good. *(Al-Ahzab, 33:29)*

God has promised forgiveness and a rich reward to those who have faith and do good works. *(Al-Ma'ida, 5:9)*

Say, '[God says], My servants who have harmed yourselves by your own excess, do not despair of God's mercy. God forgives all sins: He is truly the Most Forgiving, the Most Merciful.' *(Al-Zumar, 39:53)*

Hurry towards your Lord's forgiveness and a Garden as wide as the heavens and earth prepared for the righteous, who give, both in prosperity and

---

152 Or 'We sent you [Prophet] only as a mercy to all people'.

adversity, who restrain their anger and pardon people – God loves those who do good. *(Al-'Imran, 3:133-134)*

[Believers], do not allow your oaths in God's name to hinder you from doing good, being mindful in everything of God and making peace between people. God hears and knows everything. *(Al-Baqara, 2:224)*

Peace

The servants of the Lord of Mercy are those who walk humbly on the earth, and who, when aggressive people address them, reply, with words of peace. *(Al-Furqan, 25:63)*

A light has now come to you from God, and a Scripture making things clear, with which God guides to the ways of peace those who follow what pleases Him, bringing them from darkness out into light, by His will, and guiding them to a straight path. *(Al-Ma'ida, 5:15-16)*

He is ever merciful towards the believers – When they meet Him, they will be greeted with 'Peace' – and He has prepared a generous reward for them. *(Al-Ahzab, 33:43-44)*

But if they incline towards peace, you [Prophet] must also incline towards it, and put your trust in God: He is the All Hearing, the All Knowing. *(Al-Anfal, 8:61)*

Faithfulness to treaties, justice and moderation in conflict

But as for those who reach people with whom you have a treaty, or who come over to you because their hearts shrink from fighting against you or against their own people, God could have given them power over you, and they would have fought you. So if they withdraw and do not fight you, and offer you peace, then God gives you no way against them. *(Al-Nisa', 4: 90)*

Fulfil any pledge you make in God's name and do not break oaths after you have sworn them, for you have made God your surety: God knows everything you do. Do not use your oaths to decive each other – like a woman who unravels the thread she has firmly spun – just because one party may be more numerous than another. God tests you with this, and on the Day of the Resurrection He will make clear to you those things you differed about. *(Al-Nahl, 16:91-92)*

Do not let your hatred for the people who barred you from the Sacred Mosque induce you to break the law: help one another to do what is right and good; do not help one another towards sin and hostility. Be mindful of God, for His punishment is severe. *(Al-Ma'ida, 5:2)*

You who believe, be steadfast in your devotion to God and bear witness impartially: do not let hatred of others[153] lead you away from justice, but adhere to justice, for that is closer to awareness of God. Be mindful of God: God is well aware of what you do. *(Al-Ma'ida, 5:8)*

---

153 This resumes the instruction in vv.1-2.

Appendix 3: *Hadiths* that relate to dialogue

O people! Remember that your Lord is one, your father is one. An Arab is
not superior over a non-Arab nor a non-Arab is superior over an Arab; also a
white is not superior over a black nor a black is superior over a white except
by *taqwa* (piety, Godfearing).
(Abu `Abd Allah Ahmad ibn Muhammad ibn Hanbal al-Shaybani, *Musnad*,
vol.5, 411)

[After the conquest of Mecca the Prophet (pbuh) dealt with the Meccans,
who had cruelly persecuted the Muslims for years, in the following way:] 'O,
people of Quraish! What do expect me to do with you?' They replied: 'Peace,
a gracious brother and a son of a gracious brother!' The Prophet said: 'I will
say to you what Joseph said to his brothers before: "This day let no reproach
be upon you! Go! You are free."'
(Abu Muhammad 'Abd al-Malik ibn Hisham, *As-Sirah an-Nabawiyyah*,
vol.2, 274)

A person who works for the good of widows and the helpless is like those
who fight in the name of Allah
(Muhammad ibn Isma'il al-Bukhari, *Sahih al-Bukhari*)

The most virtuous *jihad* is speaking truth to a despotic and tyrannical ruler's
face.
(Abu Dawud al-Sijistani, *Sunan Abu Dawud*, Melahim, hadith no. 17)

Prophet Muhammad (may peace be upon Him) said: 'I am most akin to the
son of Mary among the whole of mankind, and the Prophets are of different
mothers, but of one religion, and no Prophet was raised between Me and
Him (Jesus).'
(Al-Bukhari, *Sahih Bukhari*, hadith no. 651; Muslim ibn al-Hajjaj, *Sahih
Muslim*, hadith nos. 5,8,3,4)

Prophet Muhammad (pbuh) said: 'A believer is not a fault-finder and is not
abusive, obscene, or coarse.'
(Muhammad b. 'Isa al Tirmidhi, *Jami al-Tirmidhi*, Birr, hadith no. 48)

Prophet Muhammad (pbuh) said: 'The most perfect believer is one who
has excellent manners; and the best among you are those who behave best
towards their wives.'

(Abu 'Abdillah Muhammad ibn Yazid ibn Majah, *Sunan ibn Majah,* Niqah, hadith no. 50; 'Abd Allah ibn 'Abd al-Rahman Al-Darimi, *Sunan al-Darimi,* Niqah, hadith no. 55)

Prophet Muhammad (pbuh) said: 'Each person's every joint must perform an act of charity each day the sun comes up: to act justly between two people is a form of charity; to help a man with his mount, lifting him on or hoisting up his belongings is a charity: a good word is a charity, every step towards prayer is a charity and removing a harmful thing from the road is a charity.'
(Al-Bukhari, *Sahih Bukhari,* Adab, hadith no. 870; Muslim, *Sahih Muslim,* Fada'il)

Prophet Muhammad (pbuh) said: 'If someone seeks refuge in God, give him refuge. If someone asks in the name of God, give Him something. If someone does you a favour, repay him. If you cannot find anything to repay him, then pray for him so that he knows that you appreciate what he has done for you.'
(Abu Dawud, *Sunan Abu Dawud,* Zakah, hadith no. 38; Ahmad ibn Shu'ayb ibn Alī ibn Sīnān Abū 'Abd ar-Ra-mān al-Nasa'i, *Sunan an-Nasa'i,* Zakah, hadith no. 72)

Prophet Muhammad (pbuh) said: 'Those who show no mercy to others will have no mercy shown to them by God.'
(Muslim, *Sahih Muslim,* Fada'il, hadith no. 66; al Tirmidhi, *Jami al-Tirmidhi,* Birr, hadith no. 16)

The God-fearing believers shall be against the rebellious or him who seeks to spread injustice, or sin or animosity, or corruption between believers; the hand of every man shall be against him even if he be a son of one of them.
(Medina Charter, Article 13 (see Appendix 1))

Prophet Muhammad (pbuh) said: 'Do not spread hatred or envy among yourselves and do not conspire. Rather, O Servants of God, be brothers.'
(Al-Bukhari, *Sahih Bukhari,* Adab, hadith nos. 57, 58)

A man asked the Prophet (pbuh): 'What sort of deeds or (what qualities of) Islam are good?' The Prophet (pbuh) replied: 'To feed (the poor) and greet those whom you know and those whom you do not know.'
(Al-Bukhari, *Sahih Bukhari,* Iman, hadith no. 11)

Prophet Muhammad (pbuh) said: 'Gabriel continued to press me so much about treating neighbours kindly and politely that I thought he would order me to make them my heirs.'
(Al-Bukhari, *Sahih Bukhari*, Adab, hadith no. 43)

Prophet Muhammad (pbuh) said: 'One who believes in God and the Last Day should do good to his guests. One who believes in God and the Last Day should do good to his neighbours. One who believes in God and the Last Day should say something good, or keep silent.'
(Al-Bukhari, *Sahih Bukhari*, Adab, hadith no. 31; Muslim, *Sahih Muslim*, Iman, hadith no. 74)

Prophet Muhammad (pbuh) said: 'Fear God wherever you are, and follow up a bad deed with a good one and it will wipe it out, and behave well towards people.'
(Al Tirmidhi, *Jami al-Tirmidhi*, Birr, hadith no. 55)

Prophet Muhammad (pbuh) said: 'Don't consider me superior to Moses. All people will become unconscious (on the Day of Resurrection) and I will be the first to gain consciousness to see Moses standing and holding a side of God's Throne. I will not know whether he gained consciousness before me, or if he were amongst those whom God had exempted (from unconsciousness in the first place).'
(Al-Bukhari, *Sahih Bukhari*, book 56, hadith no. 620)

Prophet Muhammad (pbuh) said: 'A Muslim is the one who avoids harming others with his tongue and his hands.'
(Al-Bukhari, *Sahih Bukhari*, al-Riqaq, hadith no. 491)

Prophet Muhammad (pbuh) said: 'Be kind, for whenever kindness becomes a part of something, it beautifies it; wherever it is taken from something, it leaves it tarnished.'
(Muslim, *Sahih Muslim*, Birr, hadith nos. 7, 8; Abu Dawud, *Sunan Abu Dawud*, Adab, hadith no. 11)

Prophet Muhammad (pbuh) said: 'By Him in Whose Hand is my life, if you were not (capable) to commit sin, God would sweep you out of existence and He would replace you with people who would commit sin, then seek forgiveness from God, and then God would forgive them.'
(Muslim, *Sahih Muslim*, Kitab al-Tauba, hadith nos. 6621, 6622)

Prophet Muhammad (pbuh) said: 'A woman went to Hell because of a cat she had tied up, not letting it eat or freeing it so that it could feed itself on rodents, until the cat died.'
(Muslim, *Sahih Muslim,* Birr, hadith no. 169)

On another occasion, Prophet Muhammad (pbuh) said: 'A sinful person saw a dog moving around a well on a hot day, hanging out its tongue in thirst. This person drew water from the well in her shoe and gave it to the dog. (For this act) she was pardoned.'
(Al-Bukhari, *Sahih Bukhari,* book 3, hadith no. 322)

Mujahid reported that a sheep was slaughtered for 'Abdullah ibn 'Amr. He asked his slave, 'Have you given any to our Jewish neighbour? Have you given any to our Jewish neighbour? I heard the Messenger of Allah, may Allah bless him and grant him peace, say, "Jibril kept on recommending that I treat my neighbours well until I thought that he would order me to treat them as my heirs."'[154]
(Al-Bukhari, *al-Adab al-Mufrad,* 'Neighbours', hadith no. 105.)

---

154 The translation used is by Ustadha Aisha Bewley; see: 'Neighbours; Al-Adab al-Mufrad Al-Bukhari', SunniPath website, accessed 30th November 2011, http://www.sunnipath.com/library/Hadith/H0003P0006.aspx.